ACKNOWLEDGEMENT

I am deeply indebted to my loving, awesome heavenly FATHER (God), who has been so faithful through all generations. I am keenly aware that I am nothing and can do nothing of myself without the creator, John 3:27 *"A man can receive nothing except it be given him from heaven".*

If this book is a blessing to every Christian particularly workers in His vineyard, it is because of God. *"What hast thou that thou didst not receive?"* (1Corinthians 4:7).

I also appreciate my late husband- Sunday Olanipekun Sokan, my children and grandchildren; they all add so much to my life experiences.

I specially and most importantly with utmost humility and reverence appreciate Prophet (Dr.) Adebowale Adedeji and his wife Lady Apostle Olufunsho Adedeji who out of their tight schedule deemed it fit to find time to pen down the first word.

Pastor Opeyemi Sokan - for final editing, arrangement, proof reading and review of the manuscript and constructive suggestions. I am very grateful.

To 'Seun Sokan - a busy father, for designing the cover page of the book, encouragement and offering useful suggestions. I remain grateful.

And others who have contributed to the successful completion of this book, I appreciate you all.

May God Almighty continue to increase all of you from all corners of the world and may all our Youths be light and worthy ambassadors to the world in Jesus name.

Amen

DEDICATION

This book **"Cries from the heart"** is dedicated to Late Prophet Gabriel Olubunmi Fakeye. I appreciate your tutelage about the basics of the effective use of Psalms for prayers, Praises and worship to God. You were a great mentor and an amiable role model. Your encouragement and influence in my life has been priceless. You will forever be remembered. Continue to Rest in the bosom of the LORD.

I cannot but mention my loving late husband, Sunday Olanipekun Sokan; for his love. You were a peaceful, disciplined, worthy husband and father to our children. Thanks for all your encouragement, support and timely advice you gave me for the success of my ministry. Your memory still lingers on in the mind of your children and l. Continue to Rest in peace with the LORD.

Both Prophet Gabriel Olubunmi Fakeye and Sunday Olanipekun Sokan (My late husband) will forever be remembered for the spiritual legacy of having Christ as the Lord, Savior and foundation of one's life. The Yoruba adage says, *'didun didun ni iranti eni rere ati olododo'* (meaning, *'worthy is the pleasant memories of an honorable, disciplined and honest man'*).

This dedication will not be complete without the mention of all the **Prophets and Pastors** who have in one way or the other been useful through their ministries by supporting the course of this insightful write up on the book of Psalms. I appreciate you all.

THE BOOK OF PSALMS
PREFACE

God listens, appreciates and gives songs to His peoples; hence we ought and in fact should continually sing unto the LORD most high for His marvelous and wondrous deeds to us.

It is in this frame of singing joyfully unto the LORD, that we show how happy we are, who God is, how appreciative, sad and sorrowful we are .in fact our songs exhibit the situation in which we are.

Through our songs, people can depict the type of spirit in us, either spiritually filled or satanic filled. May we not be filled with the demonic spiritual songs in Jesus' name. Amen.

In singing to God, we have spiritual fullness of joy in HIM for we are filled with the Holy Spirit. This enriches us with wisdom, thankful hearts and understanding. Whoever has a thankful heart will appreciate the living God, the Almighty, the El-Shaddai, the I AM that IAM, the creator of the universe.

Such a grateful person will live a life worthy of the LORD and will strive to please HIM (God) because he has the fullness of the Holy Spirit. (Colossians 1:10).

In the book of Ephesians 5:19, Paul the Apostle admonished us to sing unto the LORD and speak to 'ourselves' in psalms and spiritual songs and even make melody in our hearts to the LORD God.
David, the psalmist was and is still an exemplary example of a spirit filled man that sang to the LORD God.

David was a man that had great potentials to be a musician, warrior, king, priest, shepherd and a prophet who satisfied God in all his calling areas. He is a man that did not waste God's deposit that was in him. In fact his acts of singing psalms and songs to God became part of him. He sang anytime in joyful moments, in difficulties, in tribulations, when he was to go on assignments, when confronted with unfriendly friends, after victories were won by him, when he experienced deliverance even in repentance to God to mention but a few.

God delighted so much in him (David) and his songs that HE (God) confessed him as the man after His (God's) heart.

God made him (David) successful in all his multi-dimensional callings and ministries.

THOSE WHO SANG SONGS UNTO THE LORD

Did anybody sing to God apart from David the psalmist?

Yes! In the scriptures, there are records of those who sang songs to the LORD at various situations and for different purposes. The following are some of those who sang unto the LORD God.

1. Moses sang at the red sea (*Exodus 15*). He also sang for God's mercy (*Deuteronomy 2*).
2. The Israelites sang at Babylon for water. (*Numbers 21:17*) The Israelites also sang in respect to the fall of the wall of Jericho.
3. Deborah and Barak the son of Abinoam sang songs of praise for God's mercy and righteous deeds on behalf of Israel (*Judges 5*).

4. Hannah sang to celebrate God's providential care. She also rejoiced in His salvation for God is Holy and HE alone is God. (*I Samuel 2; Psalm 13:5-6*).
5. Mary sang songs in the house of Zachariah on her visit to Elizabeth when she heard the testimony of Elizabeth's babe leaping for joy in the mother's womb at the greetings of Virgin Mary. (*Luke 1:46-55; I Samuel 2, 1-10*).
6. Zachariah himself sang songs at the circumcision and naming of John the Baptist, (*Luke1:68-79*).
7. Simeon and Anna (who was waiting for the consolation of Israel saw Jesus before he died) sang in the temple on the eight days of Jesus Christ at his dedication. Their song on this glorious occasion was to praise God for giving both them the grace to see Jesus Christ the savior of the world before they died as they were very old.

(**Note:** Anna was a prophetess, the daughter of Phamuel of the tribe of Aser. She was a widow of four scores and four years (84 years) who lived in the temple at that time and served God with fasting and prayers night and day).

8. Those who did not abandon their faith in Christ when persecuted, threatened or killed by anti-Christ sang songs in the presence of God, the 'Songs of Moses', songs of the lamb and songs of triumph. (*Revelation 5, 9-end; and Revelation 7: 9-12.*

At the end of Jesus Christ ministry and journey on earth; to bring all His activities to an end with His disciples Jesus took the last supper with them.

It is interesting and worthy of note that Christ the Lord took 'a hymn' together with them (the disciples). At this period, HE (JESUS) was out to embark on His most difficult assignment - a journey to the cross.

Having Jesus Christ set an example for us; in singing hymns with His disciples, it is good to sing songs, psalms, hymns, choruses unto the LORD regularly.

It is very unfortunate that a lot of believers and Christians attribute the use or singing of PSALMS in particular to the 'Cherubim and Seraphim Churches and Celestial Churches of Christ denominations alone.

However, these denominations do use the psalms regularly in their worship.

You may ask 'Why is this so'? This is because they have chosen 'a good heritage' and the lines have fallen unto them in pleasant places as for the use of Psalms (Psalm 16:6).

Nevertheless, all believers as children of God and joint heirs with Christ should emulate David and Jesus Christ in singing songs, hymns, psalms, choruses, etc for God's delight in this.

The brief piece of writings on the book of PSALMS is to expose us to the purpose, uses and how we can learn to sing unto the LORD in all situations we may find ourselves - joyful, sorrowful, on assignments, in battles, during victories, seeking and having deliverances for God gives songs and is delighted in our hymns, songs psalms, choruses and praises.

The book of Revelations also confirms that angels in heaven sing round the throne of God.

As you go through this piece of writing on the book of PSALMS, may God open your eyes to the mysteries and blessings of these PSAMLTERS and hymns for your salvation. May HE (God) also give you a beautiful and joyous song to sing for His praise. Amen.

PHASE ONE

INTRODUCTION

Song:

1. My hope is built on nothing else
   Than Jesus blood and righteousness
   No merit of my own I claim
   But wholly lean on Jesus' name.
   Chorus: *On Christ, the solid rock, I stand,*
   All other ground is sinking sand (2ce).

2. When long appears my boil some race
   I rest on His unchanging grace
   In every high and stormy gale
   My anchor holds within the veil
   Chorus: *On Christ, the solid rock, I stand,*
   All other ground is sinking sand (2ce)

3. His Oath, His covenant, and blood
   Support me in the whelming flood;
   When every earthly propos gives way,
   He then is all my hope and stay.
   Chrous: *On Christ, the solid rock, I stand,*

All other ground is sinking sand (2ce)

4. When the last trumpet's voice shall sound,
   Oh may I then in Him be found
   robbed in His righteousness alone
   Faultless to stand before the throne,
   Chorus: *On Christ, the solid rock, I stand,
   All other ground is sinking sand(2ce)* Amen.

In the journey of my life, in my darkest hours and at my cross roads, when the help of man became very rare and an essential commodity, when it was only mockery, blackmail and discouragement, I found help and direction in God through the inspiration of the songs of the psalmist whose journey and pattern of prayers, trust and hope with firm faith in God showed me light.

David's prayers on each occasion of his life's affliction lead me to biblical hope.

THE BELIEVERS BIBLICAL HOPE

Biblical 'hope serves the inspiration of our 'hearts cries' unto God almighty Often when we are afflicted, we look up unto God by praying and expressing our heart desires for deliverance to God. Hence Ps.34:18-19, says *"the LORD is high unto them that are of broken heart; and saveth such as be of a contrite spirit. Many are the afflictions of the righteous; but the LORD delivereth him out of them all"*.

With the realization that the LORD God is high and can give help beyond that of his creation (man), the broken heart saddled with afflictions makes a 'cry' unto him for total deliverance.

Without biblical hope there can be no 'cry'. Then what then is **Biblical hope**?

The nature of hope, concerns the future (*Rom. 8:25*) Hope is a wishful thinking about something good happening in the future. Biblical hope then is a firm confidence from God about future issues because they are based on God's promises and revelation. In other words biblical hope which is hoping in God can be or is linked inseparably to a firm faith (*Rom. 15:13; Heb.11:1*) and confident trust in God (*Ps. 33:21-22*).

These two work together for a glorious result. David, the psalmist makes it clear to us in his songs when he uses (parallels) "trust" and "hope" and he said

"Put not your trust in princes, nor in the son of man, in whom there is no help……..happy is he that hath the God of Jacob for his help, whose hope is in the LORD his God"(Ps. 146:3-5, Jer.17:7).

Consequently the sure hope of the believer is a hope that "maketh not ashamed" (*Rom. 5:5, Ps. 22:4-5; Isaiah 49;23*).

"Which hope we have as an anchor of the soul, both sure and steadfast, and which entereth into that within vail.

THE BASIS OF BELIEVERS CONFIDENT HOPE

If hope is an anchor for the believer, what are the bases?

The foundation or the believers' confident hope is derived from the nature of God, of Jesus Christ and of God's word.

In other words, firstly scripture reveals how God has proved Himself faithful in the past on behalf of His people. For instance, the exodus of the Israelites from. Egypt (*Exodus 14 and 25*), David's struggle with a personal situation that threatened his life, when he reflected on God's actions in the past. He (David) felt confident that God will deliver him and he said, "Our father trusted in thee, they trusted and thou didst deliver them". *(Ps.22:4)*.

In addition, the full revelation of the new covenant in Jesus Christ provides even more reasons for a confident hope in God. For believers, the Son of God comes to destroy the work of the devil *(I John 3:8)*.

By his death and resurrection HE shattered the power of Satan's realm *(John 12:31)* and exhibited the power of God's kingdom which is God's power in action in the world, His spiritual rule on earth in the hearts of and among his people *(John 14:23; Is 64:1 Mark 9:1; I Cor. 4:20)*. Hence, Peter exclaims regarding our hope *"Blessed be the God and father of our Lord Jesus Christ, which according to his abundant mercy hath begotten us again unto lively hope by the resurrection of Jesus Christ from Dead"*.

Jesus is therefore called our hope *(Col.1:27; I Tim.1:1)*. We must set our hope on him through the power of the Holy Spirit *(Rom. 15:12-13; I Pet. 1:13)*

Furthermore, God's word is the third basis of hope. God revealed His WORD through Prophets and

Apostles of old, whom he inspired by the Holy Spirit to write and speak without error (*Psalm 119:49, 74, 81,114,147; Ps.130:5; Acts 26:6; Rom.15:4*). In fact everything we know about God, Jesus Christ - his son and the Holy Spirit is revealed in the infallible scriptures.

Through the above three basic foundations, the believers confident hope is established. Therefore, the believer's ultimate hope and trust must not be in other human beings (*Ps. 3316-17; 47; 10-11*), or in material possessions or money (*Ps. 20:7; Matt.6:9-21; Luke 2:13-21; 1 Tim. 6:17; Numbers 18:20.*).

Our hope is in these seven areas.

1. Our hope is based on God's love and God's grace in the midst of the sufferings we undergo in our present lives (*Psalms 33:18-19; 42:1-5; 71;1-5,13-14; Jeremiah.17:17-18*).

2. We as believers have our hope that the time will come when our sufferings on earth will be finally done away with, when the subjection of the earth to corruption will end and when the redemption

(resurrection) of our bodies will occur (*Romans 8:18-25; Psalm 16:9-10; II Peter 3:12*).
3. We have the hope of the consummation of our salvation (*I Thess. 5:8*).
4. We have the hope of an eternal house in the new heaven (*II Cor. 5:1-5; II Peter 3:13; John 14:2*) and in that city whose builder and maker is God (*Hebrews 11:10*).
5. We, as believers have blessed hope of the glorious appearing of our Great God and Savior Jesus Christ (*Titus 2:13*) when believers will be caught up from the earth to meet him in the clouds (*I Thess. 4:13-18*).
6. We have the hope of receiving a crown of righteousness (*II Timothy 4:8*) of Glory (*I Peter 5:4*) and of Life (*Revelation 2:10*).
7. Finally, we as believers have the hope of eternal life (*Titus 1:2; 3:7*); the life guaranteed to all who trust and obey the Lord Jesus Christ. (*John 3:16, 36; 6:47; I John 5:11-13*).

Being aware of such great promises from God, and His son Jesus Christ, our focus should entirely be on the creator, the author and finisher of life for our survival, deliverance and salvation. Nothing must distract or separate us from God, rather our sufferings and affliction should draw us closer to God, the way David the psalmist did. He was and is a good and great example. Of course, he was a man after the "heart of God". History recorded and had it that God loved and still loves him. Why David was the man after God's heart the steps he took when he was in trouble and great affliction?

Come with me in this little exposition of the book of Psalms to see how we can relate with God, what we can do to get closer to him in affliction and to revive our "hope" and 'trust' in God with unshakable faith. 'Who shall separate us from the love of Christ'? (*Romans 8:35-39*) nor any other creature shall be able to separate us from the love of God.

As you study the book of Psalms, may God Almighty grant you wisdom and understanding to let you see, perceive and receive His blessings and your deliverance and victory from all categories of affliction in Jesus name. Amen.

Can you remember instances of David's sober '*cries from the heart*' unto the Lord God?

PHASE TWO
THE BOOK OF PSALMS

BRIEF HISTORY

The Book of Psalms comprises of one hundred and fifty spiritual songs and poems used by the church in all ages in worship and devotional exercises. It was used as the hymn-book of the second temple.

The predominant themes are PRAYER and PRAISE, but the psalms cover a great variety of religious experiences. They are quoted more frequently in the New Testament than any other book except Isaiah.

They are often called the *'Psalms of David'* because he was the author of a large number of them. The psalms were believed to have been largely written between the 5th and 10th century B.C.

The earliest known psalms were from Moses in the 15th century B.C. (i.e. Psalm 90), the latest ones are from the 6th to 5th centuries B.C. (e.g. Psalm 137).

The majority of the psalms, however, were written in the 10th century B.C. during Israel's golden age of poetry.

AUTHORSHIP

The authorship of many of the chapters is uncertain; it is possible that in some cases the name affixed to certain psalms may refer to the collector rather than the author.

The following is a conjectural list of authors taken from the various versions of the Bible. These are Biblical or historical references of psalms that are attributed to the followings authors:

David -	73 Chapters
Sons of Korah –	11 Chapters
Asaph –	12 Chapters
Heman –	1 Chapter
Ethan –	1 Chapter
Solomon –	2 Chapters
Moses –	1 Chapter
Haggai –	1 Chapter
Zechariah –	1 Chapter

Hezekiah – Number of chapters is doubtful

Ezra – 1 Chapter

Anonymous – The remaining referred to as 'the anonymous Psalms' are about fifty in number and are referred to as *"Orphan psalms"*

With the exception of Moses, David and Solomon, all other designated authors were priests or heavies with musical gifts and responsibilities, sacred worship during David's reign.

Each of these authors was involved at different stages in the collection of the psalms for corporate use in Jerusalem.

The last or final compiling of the Psalter most likely occurred during the time of Ezra and Nehemiah.

MESSIANIC PSALMS

These are psalms which are regarded as containing direct or typical references to Christ. They refer to:

1. Christ as king – (Psalms 45, 72,110; 132:11).

2. The sufferings of Christ –(Psalms 22, 41, 55:12-14; 69:20 – 21).

3. The resurrection of Christ – (Psalm 16).

4. The Ascension of Christ – (Psalm 68:18).

TOPICAL ARRANGEMENTS

Each psalm is arranged under some topics which appear prominently in it. Such as:

I. MAN

    a. Exaltation – (Psalm 8)

    b. Sinfulness – (Psalm 10, 14,36,55,59, e.t.c.)

II. THE WORLDLY AND WICKED

    a. Contrasted with godly – (Psalms 1, 4, 5)

    b. The delay of punishment of the wicked – (Psalm 10)

    c. The Prosperity of the wicked – (Psalms 37, 73)

    d. The fate of – (Psalms 9, 11)

    e. Trust in riches – (Psalm 49)

III. RELIGIOUS EXPERIENCES

    a. Penitence – (Psalms 25, 38, 51,130)

    b. Pardon – (Psalm 32)

    c. Conversion - (Psalm 40)

    d. Trust – (Psalms 3,16,20,23,27,31,34,42,61,62,91,121)

    e. Consecration - (Psalm 116)

    f. Teachablility- (Psalm 25)

    g. Aspiration – (Psalms 42, 63,143)

    h. Prayer – (Psalms 55, 70, 77, 85, 86,142,143)

    i. Praise - Psalm 96, 98,100,103,107,136,145,148, 138, 149,150

    j. Worship – (Psalms 43, 84,100,122,132)

    k. Affiliation – (Psalms 6, 13, 22, 69, 88, 102)

    l. Old-Age – (Psalm 71)

    m. Vanity of life – (Psalms 39, 49, 90)

    n. Home – (Psalm 127)

    o. Home sickness typical- (Psalms 137)

IV. THE CHURCH (TYPICAL)

    a. Safety of – (Psalm 46)

    b. Glory of the church – (Psalms 48, 87)

    c. Love for the church – (Psalms 84, 122)

    d. Unity in the church – (Psalm 133)

V. THE WORD OF GOD – (Psalms 19, 119)

VI. **MISSIONARY** – (Psalms 67, 72, 96, 98)

VII. **DUTY OF RULERS** – (Psalms 82,101)

VIII. **DIVINE ATTRRIBUTES:**

a. Wisdom, Majesty, Greatness and Power – (Psalms 18, 19, 29, 62, 66, 89, 93, 97, 99, 118, 147).
b. Mercy (Forgiveness) – (Psalms 32, 51 85, 136).
c. Infinite knowledge – (Psalm 139).
d. Creative power– (Psalms 33, 89,104).

IX. ISRAEL'S EXPERIENCES

a. Unbelief – (Psalm 78).
b. Desolation and misery - (Psalms 79, 80).
c. Backsliding– (Psalm 81)
d. Divine providence –(Psalms 105,106,114).

GOD AS SEEN IN THE BOOK OF PSALMS

The psalmists view God in a rich variety of ways; as a Fortress, Rock, Shield, Shepherd, Victor, Creator, Ruler, Judge, Redeemer, Sustainer, Healer, and Avenger.

The psalmists see God as one that expresses love, anger, compassion and He is everywhere present, all knowing and Almighty. His greatness and power is supreme.

GOD'S PEOPLE

The description of God's people in the book of psalms cannot be overlooked, they are seen as the apple of His (God's) eyes, sheep, saints, the upright, the righteous, whom HE has brought out of horrible situation and has set their feet on a rock and given them a new song to sing.

God also directs his peoples' footsteps, satisfies their spiritual longings, forgives all their sins, disciplines and corrects their mistakes, heals all their diseases and provides for them an eternal dwelling.

What a marvelous, merciful, loving and caring father God is to His entire people.

At the very center of the BIBLE are songs, rising up like a tune from its heart. These songs capture the innermost thoughts and prayers of Old Testament people and they still speak directly to our needs today. For every emotions, mood, situation, and circumstances, you can find a psalm to match. The psalms wrestle with the deepest sorrow and ask God the hardest questions about suffering and injustice. Their voice is refreshingly spontaneous. They do not tip flowery compliments towards God; they cry out to HIM or shout for joy before HIM.

Try to read through the PSALMS. After you might have read through the poems; referred to as psalms, you cannot think of the Old Testament as dry and rule bound nor can you see the Old Testament God distant and impersonal neither has HE changed in the New Testament or in this present age.

In almost every psalm, you find the presence of God as an active, strong, loving ruler - a God who makes a difference in life.

HOW THE PSALMS CAME TOGETHER

A number of poets and writers contributed to the writing of the book of psalms and about a third of it (Psalms) are completely written by anonymous authors, while almost half of these psalms are credited to David, but at least one psalm was recorded written five hundred (500) years after David's birth.

How the psalms did come together? They seem to have been compiled as a hymn book for use in temple worship. Some psalms were written from individual's experiences but were adapted for congregational use. Directions for musicians were added along with a few verses to widen the psalms meaning for everybody.

The psalms show tremendous variation reflecting the many personalities who contributed their poems and prayers over several centuries. Yet, readers have found an inner consistency in the whole book, so they can move from one psalm to the next without being particularly aware that one poem is centuries older than another. Some have called the psalms "*a bible within the bible*" – different books telling a single story.

Other schools of thought have compared the book of psalms to a beautiful church auditorium or cathedral built over centuries with each wing and window showing the individual geniuses of its designers; yet all the parts are somewhat harmonious. This harmony comes not merely from a common sense of style but from unity of purpose; which the whole church/cathedral/auditorium is made for worship of one and the same God. Just so, the psalms reflect in a hundred moods, experiences, and the never-changing reality of a strong and loving God who cares for His people.

THE PRESENCE OF REAL ENEMIES

In the Psalms, God is not the only reality, equally persistent are enemies who sneer hurt and plot violence. They (enemies) too appear in nearly every psalm.

For the psalmists, 'faith in God' was a struggle against powerful forces that often seemed more real than God.

The writers and authors of the book of Psalms frequently asked, "Where are you, God?; Why are you far from me?; 'Why don't you help me'?; to mention but a few of those questions. Despite their love for God, they often felt abandoned, misused, and betrayed. They found no guarantee of safety in their closeness to God. The joy and praise that saturated these prayers came not from an absence of problems but from a deep conviction that a great God would overcome them.

Jesus' dying on the cross, twice expresses himself in the words of psalms (*Psalm 22:1 and 31:5*), and His disciples, in trying to explain His life, quoted from psalms more than any other book. They appear to have meditated on the psalms often as they considered the meaning of Jesus' life. In the psalms they could see that even the best men-like David - the great king suffered agony and felt abandoned.

Living by faith is not easy. It was neither for David nor for Jesus either. These powerful poems of praise and worship, some of the most beautiful ever written, offer no magical formulas to make troubles go away. Yet, while real-life questions, struggles and discouragements have a strong voice in these poems, more powerful still is the voice of *joy and security* in the strength and fortress of Israel; the LORD himself.

HOW TO STUDY PSALMS

So many of the poems called Psalms catch such deep human feelings. So the best way to study the book of psalms is to make these ancient prayers your own and speak them directly to God.

It should be noted that not all the books and chapters are attractive. Some are harsh, self-congratulatory, or boring. You may not find it easy to pray these psalms until you understand them. There are obviously a number of them..

This is the longest book in the Bible. Many people read over selected psalms, skimming over the others; but they miss the deeper messages found there, including the messages that the New-Testament writers saw when they quoted psalms more than any other Old-Testament book. The richest lessons from psalms may come from particularly difficult poems; you must read again and again until you begin to see what the author had in mind.

It is possible that you as readers may be confused by the psalmist's frequent change of voice. In a poem, the psalmist may talk to God, and then talk about HIM (GOD), then about himself (Psalmist) and then return to talking to HIM (GOD); all in rapid succession.

In the poetry of the Psalms, the form commonly used is called *parallelism,* that is, an idea is repeated using different words in the following line or lines. Parallelism in its different forms as well as the wealth of similes and metaphors lend charm and beauty to Hebrew poetry. This seems to be strange English prose but was common in Hebrew poetry. In fact most of the psalms can make perfect sense if you can give 'Time' and 'close attention' to them.

The **Psalms** were used by Jesus, who sang and quoted them several times. The writers of the New Testament quote from the Psalms more than a hundred times. Over the centuries, the Psalms have been a source of inspiration and devotion for Christians and for the church, having been used in their worship services as well as in their outreach efforts.

You are advised at this juncture to read and re-read them, they grow richer with careful study. You as a reader will be enriched and abundantly blessed as you explore the psalms.

HELPFUL PERSPECTIVES ABOUT THE FIVE-BOOK DIVISION OF THE PSALMS

In ancient times, the book of Psalms were organized into 5 books; each living its own benedictory Psalm 150 ; not only the benediction for Book 5 but also the last chapter of the book of the psalms and a doxology for the entire Psalter.

	Book I Psalm1 - 41	Book II Psalm 42-72	Book III Psalm 73-89	Book IV Psalm 90-106	Book V Psalm 107-150
Total Psalms	41	31	17	17	44
Authorship	Mainly David	Mainly David and sons of kora	Mainly Asaph	Mainly Anonymous	Mainly David or Anonymous
Predominant Divine Name	Yahweh (the "LORD")	EL - Elohin ("God")	EL - Elohin ("God")	Yahweh (the "LORD")	Yahweh (the "LORD")
Frequent Topics	Humans and Creation	Deliverance and Redemption	Worship and Sanctuary	Deserts and God's ways	God's word and praise
Resemblance to Pentateuch	Genesis	Exodus	Levitians	Numbers	Deuteronomy

NOTE: The Sons of Korah were a Levitcal family of singers. (II Chronicles 20:19) Example is seen in Psalm 42 (one of their sons).

CHAPTER ONE
PRAISING THE GOD OF LOVE

BIBLE READING: **PSALM 1** **(King James Version)**

1 Blessed is the man that walketh not in the counsel of the ungodly, nor standeth in the way of sinners, nor sitteth in the seat of the scornful.

2 But his delight is in the law of the LORD; and in his law doth he meditate day and night.

3 And he shall be like a tree planted by the rivers of water, that bringeth forth his fruit in his season; his leaf also shall not wither; and whatsoever he doeth shall prosper.

4 The ungodly are not so: but are like the chaff which the wind driveth away.

5 Therefore the ungodly shall not stand in the judgment, nor sinners in the congregation of the righteous.

6 For the LORD knoweth the way of the righteous: but the way of the ungodly shall perish.

PURPOSE: Working in the righteous way of God enhances God's blessings.

This psalm is of two natures; the first is being blessed of God (verse 1) while the second is being blown in the wild (verses 1 to 4).

Here are both negative and positive conditions of being blessed of God. It is of great importance where we walk, stand or sit. (Verse 1). Why? The different types of company mentioned in this verse can be of evil influence in our lives.

i. Counsel of the wicked?

ii. Sinners?

iii. Mockers?

It is imperative that an individual whether male or female, young or old, rich or poor, who walk in the counsel of the wicked; stand in the way of sinners and sit in the seat of mockers will be influenced negatively? It is very necessary for us to keep our tune with God's word each day as a regular habit.

This however is a positive step towards been blessed by God. The reward to be expected is worth the effort.

Verse 3 says, *"The blessed man is liken to a tree planted by the streams of water that yields its fruits seasonally; and whose leaves does not wither. He does prosper in whatever he does"*. In considering the opposite experience of the blessed man in verse 4, the wicked man is likened to CHAFF. Chaff, however, can look stable and settled until the wind begins to blow.

The opposite of 'a tree planted by streams',(verse 3) should be a tree withered by drought and so it is in Jeremiah 17:5-8. This point to a similar contrast between the good and bad people. This image of the wicked as chaff" is far more absolute – a chaff is utterly worthless even for fire, it disappears in the wind.

God's judgment day is what finally makes the wicked seem like chaff. We are in the realization that there are a lot of storms in life, there is also too much risk in being counted with the chaff. We, as believers therefore, need to be careful and sensitive to our environment, the types of activities we are involved in and the relationship we make.

May we be counted worthy to be blessed in Jesus Name. Amen.

In what do you delight; and with whom are you most at ease?

PRAYER: As I walk, stand or sit every day of my life; Lord, help me to make your law my delight.

BLESSED IS THE MAN THAT WALKETH IN THE RIGHTEOUS WAY.	THE WAY OF THE UNGODLY (WICKED) SHALL PERISH PS. 1:6

CHAPTER TWO
WHY GOD LAUGHS AT CONSPIRATORS

BIBLE READING: PSALM 2 (King James Version)

Why do the heathen rage, and the people imagine a vain thing?

² The kings of the earth set themselves, and the rulers take counsel together, against the LORD, and against his anointed, saying,

³ Let us break their bands asunder, and cast away their cords from us.

⁴ He that sitteth in the heavens shall laugh: the LORD shall have them in derision.

⁵ Then shall he speak unto them in his wrath, and vex them in his sore displeasure.

⁶ Yet have I set my king upon my holy hill of Zion.

⁷ I will declare the decree: the LORD hath said unto me, Thou art my Son; this day have I begotten thee.

⁸ Ask of me, and I shall give thee the heathen for thine inheritance, and the uttermost parts of the earth for thy possession.

> ⁹ *Thou shalt break them with a rod of iron; thou shalt dash them in pieces like a potter's vessel.*
>
> ¹⁰ *Be wise now therefore, O ye kings: be instructed, ye judges of the earth.*
>
> ¹¹ *Serve the L*ORD *with fear, and rejoice with trembling.*
>
> ¹² *Kiss the Son, lest he be angry, and ye perish from the way, when his wrath is kindled but a little. Blessed are all they that put their trust in him.*

PURPOSE: Accepting to serve God in utmost fear, reverence and humility.

Israelite kings and priests were anointed with oil when they assumed office. The "Anointed One" is originally meant to be "king". It comes however to stand for more. The Hebrews believed that their king is messiah. This psalm was understood in the New Testament as referring to Jesus – for no Old Testament king ever gained the control of the nations implied here.

The conspiracy and rebellion described have a national implication for Israel, in that it is the Lord's anointed that is targeted but it is the cosmic implication that predominates. Indeed the rebellion is directed against the Lord (Verse 2). Any earthly throne, however lofty, is ultimately insecure and subject to fall. Who could have thought the fall of Late General Sanni Abacha – a onetime military dictator and tyrannical head of the Nigerian nation possible a few years ago? Even though we cannot see how today the same fate can befall the one remaining "SUPER –POWER, in fact to conspire against the throne of God is truly laughable (verse 4). No number of coups-d'état can touch the "king of kings".

In Acts 4:25-26, David's mouth, which is the channel of truth inquired about the conspiracy in unity of the heathen raged nations and the people's evil imagination. David is referring to the evil alliances of the earthly king and their rejection of God and Christ the messiah. In Acts 13:33-34, God's word is confirmed sure and that His prophecies' concerning Christ the son of God hath been fulfilled. This then is one of the "Messianic" prophecies in psalm. Hebrews 1:5 makes the point that verse 7 of Psalm 2 can only be properly understood in terms that transcend the angelic realm let alone any mere mortal kingship, and Hebrew 5:5 also ascribes the verse to Jesus Christ as Messiah. His kingdom extends far beyond the borders of Israel, (verse 8), and His power is irresistible (verse 9).

In the light of this fact, it would be most unwise to ignore the counsel in verses 10 and 11.

PRAYER: Lord, please teach me to serve you with Holy fear.

CHAPTER THREE
DELIVERANCE BELONGS TO GOD

BIBLE READING: PSALM 3 (King James Version)

Lord, how are they increased that trouble me! Many are they that rise up against me.

²Many there be which say of my soul, there is no help for him in God. Selah.

³But thou, O LORD, art a shield for me; my glory, and the lifter up of mine head.

⁴I cried unto the LORD with my voice, and he heard me out of his holy hill. Selah.

⁵I laid me down and slept; I awaked; for the LORD sustained me.

⁶I will not be afraid of ten thousands of people that have set themselves against me round about.

⁷Arise, O LORD; save me, O my God: for thou hast smitten all mine enemies upon the cheek bone; thou hast broken the teeth of the ungodly.

⁸Salvation belongeth unto the LORD: thy blessing is upon thy people. Selah.

PURPOSE: Morning Prayer for help

In this psalm, David is crying to God for help with own his son in full rebellion against him; and most of the nations deserting their kings to follow the rebel. It is not surprising that some even considered that king David was beyond help, even from God Himself. Such people do not know God. Look at the incident or miracle in verse 5, would you have been able to sleep on such an occasion? David, however, had a relationship of full confidence in God which enabled him to recognize God in the terms described in verses 3, 6, 7 and 8. Do you too know God in these terms? What he did for David, HE can and HE will do for you.

PRAYER: Thank you God for the truth in verse 3

CHAPTER FOUR

BE ANGRY, BUT SIN NOT

BIBLE READING: PSALM 4 (King James Version)

Hear me when I call, O God of my righteousness: thou hast enlarged me when I was in distress; have mercy upon me, and hear my prayer.

2 O ye sons of men, how long will ye turn my glory into shame? how long will ye love vanity, and seek after leasing? Selah.

3 But know that the LORD hath set apart him that is godly for himself: the LORD will hear when I call unto him.

4 Stand in awe, and sin not: commune with your own heart upon your bed, and be still. Selah.

5 Offer the sacrifices of righteousness, and put your trust in the LORD.

6 There be many that say, Who will shew us any good? LORD, lift thou up the light of thy countenance upon us.

7 Thou hast put gladness in my heart, more than in the time that their corn and their wine increased.

⁸I will both lay me down in peace, and sleep: for thou, LORD, only makest me dwell in safety.

PURPOSE: Evening prayer for help

It is a terrible experience to have to suffer shame not because we have done anything wrong but because people around us prefer the juicy lies to the colorless truth. (Verse 2). That is a good reason to be angry; and it is perfectly right, when situations call for it, you can be very angry indeed. In fact, Jesus our supreme example was himself very angry on an occasion. (*John 2:14-16*).

Take note that, there is a right and a wrong way to express anger as seen in verses 4 and 5 (See also *Ephesians 4:26*).

Verses 6 and 7 of this psalm refers to people who are always longing for the good times, but their concept of the good times are different from what God accords to His own servant. They do have joy and merry-making for sure, (verse 7) but even these seem to be a shallow affair and temporary peace; as what is in verse 8 does not seem to be their own lot.

PRAYER: Teach me oh Lord to be angry, but without sinning.

CHAPTER FIVE

EVIL EVERYWHERE

BIBLE READING: PSALM 5 (King James Version)

Give ear to my words, O LORD, consider my meditation.

2 Hearken unto the voice of my cry, my King, and my God: for unto thee will I pray.

3 My voice shalt thou hear in the morning, O LORD; in the morning will I direct my prayer unto thee, and will look up.

4 For thou art not a God that hath pleasure in wickedness: neither shall evil dwell with thee.

5 The foolish shall not stand in thy sight: thou hatest all workers of iniquity.

6 Thou shalt destroy them that speak leasing: the LORD will abhor the bloody and deceitful man.

7 But as for me, I will come into thy house in the multitude of thy mercy: and in thy fear will I worship toward thy holy temple.

⁸Lead me, O Lᴏʀᴅ, in thy righteousness because of mine enemies; make thy way straight before my face.

⁹For there is no faithfulness in their mouth; their inward part is very wickedness; their throat is an open sepulchre; they flatter with their tongue.

¹⁰Destroy thou them, O God; let them fall by their own counsels; cast them out in the multitude of their transgressions; for they have rebelled against thee.

¹¹But let all those that put their trust in thee rejoice: let them ever shout for joy, because thou defendest them: let them also that love thy name be joyful in thee.

¹²For thou, Lᴏʀᴅ, wilt bless the righteous; with favour wilt thou compass him as with a shield.

PURPOSE: A Morning Prayer

Renowned for their beautiful pictures of God's love, the psalms present equally heartfelt portraits of evil. They often describe people who deeply deserve God's punishment.

In Romans 3:10-18, Paul quotes from a number of different Psalms like this one (*Psalm 5*) making his case that "evil" infects all people everywhere.

Firmly determined to seek God with all his heart, David committed himself to God via these three actions:

i. Confidence that God will hear his voice, he will persist in prayer and not live without it (*Verses 1 and 2; Deuteronomy 4:29*).

ii. He will pray to God "in the morning". If we orient our lives around God, morning prayers will be the natural thing to do. Each new morning calls for a renewed dedication of ourselves to God and a feeling upon His World (*Psalm119:9-16*).

iii. He (David) will "look up" in expectation for answers to his prayers and throughout the day he will search for signs that God is at work in his life.

Evil does not exist in the abstract and God detests both evil and evil doers. Hence David said in verses 5 and 6

"....thou hatest all workers of iniquity thou shall destroy them............"

God does not only hate sin, but also hates those who perpetrate evil. On the other hand, the scriptures also reveal God to be the one who loves sinners, reaches out to them in compassion and mercy, and seeks to redeem them from sin through the cross. (John 3:16).

However, the unrepentant sinner will eventually be condemned and punished by God; for He does not delight or have pleasure in wickedness. Some Psalmists solicit in this prayer for the destruction of God's enemies (the evil doers). (*Psalm 35:1-38*).

Remember that 'morning prayer' is a must for believers.

Firstly, it is to say 'thank you' to God for the peaceful night and the new dawn.

Secondly, it is to put oneself and activities to be embarked upon for the new day under God's care and protection.

Remember to start your day with the 'morning prayer' meditate on the words of this song, sing and pray them.

ANCIENT & MODERN HYMN 4; SONGS OF PRAISE HYMN 31

1. New every morning is the love
   Our wakening and uprising prove;
   Through sleep and darkness safely brought
   Restored to life, and power and thought.

2. New mercies, each returning day,
   Hover round us while we pray;
   New perils past, new sins forgiven
   New thoughts of God, new hope of heaven.

3. If on our daily course our mind,
   Be set to hallow all we find;
   New treasures still, of countless price,
   God will provide for sacrifice.

4. Old friends, old scenes will lovelier be,
   As more of heavens in each we see,
   Some softening gleam of love and prayer,
   Shall dawn on every cross and care.

5. The trivial round, the common task,

Will furnish all we need to ask,
Room to deny ourselves, a road
To bring us daily nearer God.

6. Only, O! LORD, in thy dear love,
Fit us for perfect rest above;
And help us, this and every day,
To live more nearly as we pray. Amen.

PRAYER: "Lead me, Oh LORD!, in thy righteousness because of mine enemies; make thy way straight before my face" in Jesus' name. Amen.

CHAPTER SIX
GIVE ME STRENGTH OH LORD!

BIBLE READING: PSALM 6 (King James Version)

O LORD, rebuke me not in thine anger, neither chasten me in thy hot displeasure.

²Have mercy upon me, O LORD; for I am weak: O LORD, heal me; for my bones are vexed.

³My soul is also sore vexed: but thou, O LORD, how long?

⁴Return, O LORD, deliver my soul: oh save me for thy mercies' sake.

⁵For in death there is no remembrance of thee: in the grave who shall give thee thanks?

⁶I am weary with my groaning; all the night make I my bed to swim; I water my couch with my tears.

⁷Mine eye is consumed because of grief; it waxeth old because of all mine enemies.

⁸Depart from me, all ye workers of iniquity; for the LORD hath heard the voice of my weeping.

> *⁹The LORD hath heard my supplication; the LORD will receive my prayer.*
>
> *¹⁰Let all mine enemies be ashamed and sore vexed: let them return and be ashamed suddenly.*

PURPOSE: A Prayer of Help in Times of Trouble

Psalm 6 is a cry of a sinner in distress; a sinner who knows that he deserves his troubles. This is no self righteous plea. God has good reasons to be angry and he is angry, the results of that anger are felt by the psalmist in his bones (*verse 3*). Death itself is not far away (verse 5), his grief, there are tears there and deep supplications from the heart.

Thankfully, it is not all over and all is not in vain because the Lord hears. In spite of the unworthiness of the person praying, the reason why God answers the cry is in verse 4 which says *"return O! Lord, deliver my soul, oh! save me for thy mercies sake"*. This is a reason that applies to us as well. It is for that reason that the enemy will be put to shame. The person praying also warns his enemies to depart, and he is confident that God will answer his prayer. (verses 8 to10).

a. What other truths can you discover?

b. Do you, like David, express urgent concerns and expectant faith in your prayer?

c. Do you have confident to approach God?

Hebrews 4:16 advices us as follows *"Let us have confidence, then and approach God's throne, where there is grace. There we will receive mercy and find grace to help us just when we need it"* (Good News Bible).

"Let us therefore come boldly unto the throne of grace that we may obtain mercy, and find grace to help in time of need". (KJV).

Please brethren, apply yourself in worship to David's experience of prayer and praise.

PRAYER:

Father, I bless your name and I appreciate you LORD, that you hear my prayers not because of my righteousness but because of your mercy and steadfast love. God give me confidence to approach your throne of GRACE, and there let me obtain GRACE when I am in need of it. In Jesus name I pray. Amen.

CHAPTER SEVEN
MY ENEMY: GOD'S ENEMY

BIBLE READING: **PSALM 7**

*O L*ORD *my God, in thee do I put my trust: save me from all them that persecute me, and deliver me:*

² Lest he tear my soul like a lion, rending it in pieces, while there is none to deliver.

*³ O L*ORD *my God, If I have done this; if there be iniquity in my hands;*

⁴ If I have rewarded evil unto him that was at peace with me; (yea, I have delivered him that without cause is mine enemy:)

⁵ Let the enemy persecute my soul, and take it; yea, let him tread down my life upon the earth, and lay mine honour in the dust. Selah.

*⁶ Arise, O L*ORD*, in thine anger, lift up thyself because of the rage of mine enemies: and awake for me to the judgment that thou hast commanded.*

⁷ So shall the congregation of the people compass thee about: for their sakes therefore return thou on high.

8 The Lord shall judge the people: judge me, O Lord, according to my righteousness, and according to mine integrity that is in me.

9 Oh let the wickedness of the wicked come to an end; but establish the just: for the righteous God trieth the hearts and reins.

10 My defence is of God, which saveth the upright in heart.

11 God judgeth the righteous, and God is angry with the wicked every day.

12 If he turn not, he will whet his sword; he hath bent his bow, and made it ready.

13 He hath also prepared for him the instruments of death; he ordaineth his arrows against the persecutors.

14 Behold, he travaileth with iniquity, and hath conceived mischief, and brought forth falsehood.

15 He made a pit, and digged it, and is fallen into the ditch which he made.

16 His mischief shall return upon his own head, and his violent dealing shall come down upon his own pate.

17 I will praise the Lord according to his righteousness: and will sing praise to the name of the Lord most high.

PURPOSE: A Prayer for Justice

In Psalm 7, David is experiencing persecution.

On what grounds does he make his appeal to God? David has absolute trust in God (verse 1).

It is always a good position from which to argue, knowing that one is standing in the right side.
The first five verses plead this as a fact before God. So sure is David that he dared to put his case before the All-knowing God and to do it with a curse on himself should it be in the wrong.

Are you very sure of yourself? Examine and read verses 3 to 5 again. Very rarely are we in the right to this extent, usually one side - not a hundred percent right and the other all wrong; but right and wrong are usually shared to some degree.

There are situations, however, when the enemy is not merely in error but that he has gone so far astray, that his (enemy) position amounts to heaping God's judgment on himself (*see verse 11*) .

He is not just our own enemy then, but the enemy of God himself, in which case verse 6 would be appropriate.

In what two ways does he say that judgment will overtake the wicked? (*see verses 12 and 16*).
Learn from verse 17 how prayer should end. *"I will praise the Lord accordingly to His righteousness and will sing praise to the name of the Lord most High"*

PRAYER: O Lord, my God, I take refuge in YOU. Please enable me to so walk with YOU that I will only have as enemies those who make YOU their enemy in Jesus name I pray. Amen.

CHAPTER EIGHT
THE PLACE OFMEN IN THE MIND AND PURPOSE OF GOD

BIBLE READING: PSALM 8 (King James Version)

> O LORD, our Lord, how excellent is thy name in all the earth! who hast set thy glory above the heavens.
>
> ² Out of the mouth of babes and sucklings hast thou ordained strength because of thine enemies, that thou mightest still the enemy and the avenger.
>
> ³ When I consider thy heavens, the work of thy fingers, the moon and the stars, which thou hast ordained;
>
> ⁴ What is man, that thou art mindful of him? and the son of man, that thou visitest him?
>
> ⁵ For thou hast made him a little lower than the angels, and hast crowned him with glory and honour.
>
> ⁶ Thou madest him to have dominion over the works of thy hands; thou hast put all things under his feet:

⁷ All sheep and oxen, yea, and the beasts of the field;

⁸ The fowl of the air, and the fish of the sea, and whatsoever passeth through the paths of the seas.

⁹ O LORD our Lord, how excellent is thy name in all the earth!

PURPOSE: God's Glory and Man's Dignity

This psalm is a hymn of praise in which David marvel at the majesty of God that uses the weak to overthrow the mighty (*verses 1 and 2*).

David also ponders the thought that God has entrusted His creation of the dominion of man. God's majesty not only fills the earth, but in fact extends beyond the heavens (*verses 1 and 3*). The high and mighty God chooses to value the praise of infants and suckling, to such an extent that it becomes weapon in his hands. Yet, even full-grown men (adult), what are they in comparison to the myriads of galaxies of stars running their courses way beyond the reach of our most powerful telescopes (*verse 4*) But see what glory and honour God choose to bestow on man, (*verses 5 to 8*).

In the hierarchy of the created universe, only God ranks higher than man. It is obvious to us that all animals, however fearsome, are lower than man in the creation order. What we do not often appreciate is that angels, much more powerful than we are, are usually employed by God in the service of man and never the other way round!

Reverently, there is only one answer we can give to the question in verse four, *'what is man, that thou art mindful of him? And the son of man, that thou visit him"?* Man is the supreme object of his love and grace. We do not know the reason why. We do not need to know. However, the place of man in the mind and purpose of God has been clearly declared by the Almighty himself (*See Hebrews 2:1-10*).

PRAYER: Thank you God, for the high and lofty place in which you have placed man. Please teach us to live the way you (God) intended us to live and to retain the lofty place in which you placed us in Jesus name. Amen.

CHAPTER NINE
PRAISING GOD AND CALL FOR JUSTICE

BIBLE READING: PSALM 9 (King James Version)

I will praise thee, O LORD, with my whole heart; I will shew forth all thy marvellous works.

² I will be glad and rejoice in thee: I will sing praise to thy name, O thou most High.

³ When mine enemies are turned back, they shall fall and perish at thy presence.

⁴ For thou hast maintained my right and my cause; thou satest in the throne judging right.

⁵ Thou hast rebuked the heathen, thou hast destroyed the wicked, thou hast put out their name for ever and ever.

⁶ O thou enemy, destructions are come to a perpetual end: and thou hast destroyed cities; their memorial is perished with them.

⁷ But the LORD shall endure for ever: he hath prepared his throne for judgment.

⁸ And he shall judge the world in righteousness, he shall minister judgment to the people in uprightness.

⁹ The LORD also will be a refuge for the oppressed, a refuge in times of trouble.

¹⁰ And they that know thy name will put their trust in thee: for thou, LORD, hast not forsaken them that seek thee.

¹¹ Sing praises to the LORD, which dwelleth in Zion: declare among the people his doings.

¹² When he maketh inquisition for blood, he remembereth them: he forgetteth not the cry of the humble.

¹³ Have mercy upon me, O LORD; consider my trouble which I suffer of them that hate me, thou that liftest me up from the gates of death:

¹⁴ That I may shew forth all thy praise in the gates of the daughter of Zion: I will rejoice in thy salvation.

¹⁵ The heathen are sunk down in the pit that they made: in the net which they hid is their own foot taken.

¹⁶ The LORD is known by the judgment which he executeth: the wicked is snared in the work of his own hands. Higgaion. Selah.

17 The wicked shall be turned into hell, and all the nations that forget God.

18 For the needy shall not always be forgotten: the expectation of the poor shall not perish for ever.

19 Arise, O LORD; let not man prevail: let the heathen be judged in thy sight.

20 Put them in fear, O LORD: that the nations may know themselves to be but men. Selah.

PURPOSE: Thanksgiving to God for His Justice

This Psalm nine is of two sides; it can be likened to coin.

On one side, David praises the LORD, the righteous judge, for destroying the wicked (*verses 1to 10*), he exhorts the people. On the other side, he (David) calls upon God to destroy the wicked so that the righteous may be delivered (*verses 13 to 20*).

It is worthy to note that David had many experiences in his life that are aptly captured in verse 3 and 4 and also in verses 9 and 10, and no doubt do we. Although, we are not in a position to assert in the following two verses (*11 and 12*), our desires are not for the utter ruin of our enemies, but following the teachings of our LORD, we rather wish they might turn to God and be saved.

The security that we have from God over our earthly enemies already is enough cause for praise in the manner of the first two verses of this psalm, but our eternal redemption by the one who sits on the throne (*verse 7*), calls for even more celebration of His glorious name.

Meanwhile, we live in a world where life seems to be constantly an unequal struggle between the poor, needy, the rich and powerful (*verse 17, 18*). King David's prayers in the concluding two verses of this Psalm (*verses 19 and 20*), are therefore relevant to us today.

PRAYER: "Arise O LORD; let no man prevail; let the heathen be judge in thy sight. Put them in fear, O

LORD; that they nations may know themselves to be but men. Amen

CHAPTER TEN
ARISE O LORD AND FORGET NOT THE AFFLICTED

BIBLE READING: **PSALM 10**

Why standest thou afar off, O LORD? why hidest thou thyself in times of trouble?

² The wicked in his pride doth persecute the poor: let them be taken in the devices that they have imagined.

³ For the wicked boasteth of his heart's desire, and blesseth the covetous, whom the LORD abhorreth.

⁴ The wicked, through the pride of his countenance, will not seek after God: God is not in all his thoughts.

⁵ His ways are always grievous; thy judgments are far above out of his sight: as for all his enemies, he puffeth at them.

⁶ He hath said in his heart, I shall not be moved: for I shall never be in adversity.

⁷ His mouth is full of cursing and deceit and fraud: under his tongue is mischief and vanity.

⁸ *He sitteth in the lurking places of the villages: in the secret places doth he murder the innocent: his eyes are privily set against the poor.*

⁹ *He lieth in wait secretly as a lion in his den: he lieth in wait to catch the poor: he doth catch the poor, when he draweth him into his net.*

¹⁰ *He croucheth, and humbleth himself, that the poor may fall by his strong ones.*

¹¹ *He hath said in his heart, God hath forgotten: he hideth his face; he will never see it.*

¹² *Arise, O LORD; O God, lift up thine hand: forget not the humble.*

¹³ *Wherefore doth the wicked contemn God? he hath said in his heart, Thou wilt not require it.*

¹⁴ *Thou hast seen it; for thou beholdest mischief and spite, to requite it with thy hand: the poor committeth himself unto thee; thou art the helper of the fatherless.*

¹⁵ *Break thou the arm of the wicked and the evil man: seek out his wickedness till thou find none.*

¹⁶ *The LORD is King for ever and ever: the heathen are perished out of his land.*

¹⁷ *LORD, thou hast heard the desire of the humble: thou wilt prepare their heart, thou wilt cause thine ear to hear:*

¹⁸ To judge the fatherless and the oppressed, that the man of the earth may no more oppress.

PURPOSE: A Prayer for Justice

The situation described here in Psalm ten seems like a commentary on our morning newspaper. What seems different is that, in our own situations, the wicked do not openly declare that there is no God because they know that we are a religious society; and so they pay lip service to God; but in actual fact verse 4 describes them exactly.

Like David, we are perplexed because we know that God sees them, that God is able to put an end to their arrogance, but that HE does not. As a result, they continue to prosper in their wickedness (verse 5). While the poor are crushed in their misery, and they too come to the wrong conclusion that God does not care (*verses 10 and 11*).

The response of the Psalmist was to cry to God in fervent prayers (verses 12 to 18), because he knows and cares and HE is more than able to do something about the miserable flight of the oppressed. This also should be our own response.

Make a list of the truths about the Lord in this psalm. Then try to build up a biblical principle regarding the Christian's attitude to the wicked.

PRAYER: Heavenly father, do not forget the helpless, but hear the prayers of the afflicted in Jesus name Amen.

CHAPTER ELEVEN
IN THE LORD, I TAKE REFUGE

BIBLE READING: PSALM 11 (King James Version)

*In the L*ORD *put I my trust: how say ye to my soul, Flee as a bird to your mountain?*

² For, lo, the wicked bend their bow, they make ready their arrow upon the string that they may privily shoot at the upright in heart.

³ If the foundations be destroyed, what can the righteous do?

*⁴ The L*ORD *is in his holy temple, the L*ORD*'s throne is in heaven: his eyes behold, his eyelids try, the children of men.*

*⁵ The L*ORD *trieth the righteous: but the wicked and him that loveth violence his soul hateth.*

⁶ Upon the wicked he shall rain snares, fire and brimstone, and an horrible tempest: this shall be the portion of their cup.

*⁷ For the righteous L*ORD *loveth righteousness; his countenance doth behold the upright.*

PURPOSE: A Prayer of confidence in the Lord

Psalm eleven is a song of trust in which David, among other things, expresses his faith in the Lord.

David receives good, and practical advice to flee to the mountains, (*verse 1*) because of the reason given in verse 3, *"if the foundations be destroyed, what can the righteous do?* There are times when this is the only wise thing to do. David, in fact did just that when he ran away from king Saul, and even our LORD Jesus Himself escaped (relocated) in this way on more than one occasion (*Luke 4:29-30; John 8:59*).

This however is not always an automatic or the ultimate course of action to pursue, but we must always seek the Lord's direction as to what to do at any given moment. (Read *John11: 7-10*) Seeking the Lord's direction is working with the light and walking in the light.

The basis of our confidence is in verse 4 *"The LORD is in his Holy temple, the Lord's throne is in heaven; His eyes behold, His eyelids try, the children of men"*. Our God is on the throne; so long as verse 7 is the basis of our struggle, we can always look up to HIM for guidance.

PRAYER: Oh God, teach me to know when to run away from evil and when to stand our ground in order to resist the devil. Keep me/us safe and protect me/us from wicked people in Jesus name. Amen.

CHAPTER TWELVE
SEEKING HELP FROM GOD

BIBLE READING: **PSALM 12**

*Help, L*ORD*; for the godly man ceaseth; for the faithful fail from among the children of men.*

² They speak vanity every one with his neighbour: with flattering lips and with a double heart do they speak.

*³ The L*ORD *shall cut off all flattering lips, and the tongue that speaketh proud things:*

⁴ Who have said, With our tongue will we prevail; our lips are our own: who is lord over us?

*⁵ For the oppression of the poor, for the sighing of the needy, now will I arise, saith the L*ORD*; I will set him in safety from him that puffeth at him.*

*⁶ The words of the L*ORD *are pure words: as silver tried in a furnace of earth, purified seven times.*

*⁷ Thou shalt keep them, O L*ORD*, thou shalt preserve them from this generation for ever.*

⁸ The wicked walk on every side, when the vilest men are exalted.

PURPOSE: In times of Trouble or The Evil Days

The Psalmist as a destitute of human comfort, craves help of God (verses 1 and 2), describes the evil times as it is today where exactly what is recorded/written is (in reality) really happening.

In this evil times, there are 'sins' committed universally such as murder, deceit of various forms, evil speeches, flattery (*Proverbs 20:19*); Evil words and utterances (*Job 16:3b*), boasters, arrogance (*Proverbs 8:23*), oppression (*Psalm 62:10*), etc.

The LORD promises to exalt the vilest man even when evil activities are been perpetrated by the wicked. Can any man stop God from carrying out what HE desires? Why not change from your evil ways.

PRAYER: Turn verses 6 to 8 of psalm 12 into prayer.

CHAPTER THIRTEEN
PRAYER FOR DIVINE DELAYS

BIBLE READING: **PSALM 13 (King James Version)**

How long wilt thou forget me, O LORD? forever? How long wilt thou hide thy face from me?

² How long shall I take counsel in my soul, having sorrow in my heart daily? How long shall mine enemy be exalted over me?

³ Consider and hear me, O LORD my God: lighten mine eyes, lest I sleep the sleep of death;

⁴ Lest mine enemy say, I have prevailed against him; and those that trouble me rejoice when I am moved.

⁵ But I have trusted in thy mercy; my heart shall rejoice in thy salvation.

⁶ I will sing unto the LORD, because he hath dealt bountifully with me.

PURPOSE: For help that enemy may not be exalted over one

The Psalmist prays for help that his enemies may not exalt over him. This psalm is a prayer that can and should be offered to God during prolonged trials or when there is divine delay (Psalm 35:7; 40:17).

Also when in trouble or despondency Psalm 94 is also very helpful and useful. With absolute trust in God, it is definite that you will be saved from those enemies and you will definitely rejoice in the **LORD.**

PRAYER: God remove suffering from my life and let the whole world rejoice in you for my sake in Jesus name. Amen.

God do not allow my enemies to prevail over me. Let my whole being glorify YOU forever and ever. Amen.

CHAPTER FOURTEEN
THE GENERAL CORRUPTION OF MANKIND

BIBLE READING: **PSALM 14 (King James Version)**

The fool hath said in his heart, there is no God. They are corrupt, they have done abominable works, there is none that doeth good.

² The LORD looked down from heaven upon the children of men, to see if there were any that did understand, and seek God.

³ They are all gone aside, they are all together become filthy: there is none that doeth good, no, not one.

⁴ Have all the workers of iniquity no knowledge? Who eat up my people as they eat bread, and call not upon the LORD.

⁵ There were they in great fear: for God is in the generation of the righteous.

⁶ Ye have shamed the counsel of the poor, because the LORD is his refuge.

⁷ Oh that the salvation of Israel were come out of Zion! When the LORD bringeth back the captivity of his people, Jacob shall rejoice, and Israel shall be glad.

PURPOSE: Knowing the fate of the fool

Here in this Psalm the atheist is exposed; he (Atheists) is the fool that says *"there is no God"* (*Psalm 36:1-12, Psalm 14:1; 10:4; Proverbs 30:9; Jeremiah 5:12; I John 2:22*) and will not seek him.

Psalm 10:4.describes the wicked. Many men and women are in this group; they are corrupt *"they do abominable works; there is none that doeth good"* so says verse one of Psalm 14.

The world today is of evil works and times and with men of evil hearts. Verse 3 also confirms their depravity (*Isaiah 1:6*), filthiness and universal 'sin'. Undoubtedly, there is sin everywhere - every second.

God looked down, viewed the earth from heaven and wondered if these evil men have neither knowledge nor understanding.

They are all ignorant of the existence of God. They put the poor to shame and ridicule because God is his refuge. David assures the poor who believes God of divine refuge (verses 6 and 7) that the salvation of God is certain for God's children. Restoration and great day are promised to the righteous (*verse 7, Ezra 3:12*).

Are you ready to leave your evil works, ways and words? Do it now to avoid the wrath of God Almighty. Just do what David advised in verses 2 to 5 of this Psalm 14, then you will be accepted into the Holy place by God himself.

Remember, God exists; HE is faithful, supreme and of great mercy, ready to accept anybody that repents.

The Holy sanctuary is for you and me; why defile yourself with evil works?

I join David to plead with you to leave your evil and corrupt ways and turn to God - the redeemer and restorer of life. God's Holy hill, His sanctuary awaits you for habitation; make haste don't be late.

PRAYER: LORD, look down from heaven upon me with your salvation and bring back my captivity; restore me and my family and we shall be glad in you.

God put demarcation between me, my children, my family, ministry and the entire works of the atheists in Jesus' name. Amen.

CHAPTER FIFTEEN
REQUIREMENTS FOR ACCESS INTO GOD'S SANCTUARY

BIBLE READING: PSALM 15 (King James Version)

Lord, who shall abide in thy tabernacle? who shall dwell in thy holy hill?

² He that walketh uprightly, and worketh righteousness, and speaketh the truth in his heart.

³ He that backbiteth not with his tongue, nor doeth evil to his neighbour, nor taketh up a reproach against his neighbour.

⁴ In whose eyes a vile person is contemned; but he honoureth them that fear the LORD. He that sweareth to his own hurt, and changeth not.

⁵ He that putteth not out his money to usury, nor taketh reward against the innocent. He that doeth these things shall never be moved.

PURPOSE: The happiness of the holy

In Psalm fifteen (15), David considers the requirements necessary for a person to enter the presence of God which is a sacred place. (*Deuteronomy 12:5*).

These requirements have to do with man's character and behavior not religious beliefs and observance.

The requirements for a citizen of Zion as recommend by David is that a person must be blameless and honest in his actions. In other words, the criteria for man to be accessible into God's sanctuary are righteousness, truthfulness and uprightness; must be charitable, dutiful (in positive ways) and must be free of backbiting (*Psalm 50: 20*).

The person ascribing to be in the presence of God must also despise sin, bribery and usury; for God despised the wicked and reverence those that fear HIM.

Brethren, examine yourself and make a written assessment of yourself (inclusive of your thoughts). You need to make the necessary confession of sins that come to light as soon as possible, make restitution with God. You certainly will like to enjoy lasting security that only God can give through Christ Jesus; won't you!

Take a step further by committing this to God in prayer.

PRAYER: God! My father, enable me NEVER to leave any stone unturned to seek to be in your presence daily. Amen.

CHAPTER SIXTEEN
TRUST AND CONFIDENCE IN GOD FOR PROTECTION AND PRESERVATION OF ONE'S LIFE

BIBLE READING: PSALM 16 (King James Version)

Preserve me, O God: for in thee do I put my trust.

² O my soul, thou hast said unto the LORD, Thou art my Lord: my goodness extendeth not to thee;

³ But to the saints that are in the earth, and to the excellent, in whom is all my delight.

⁴ Their sorrows shall be multiplied that hasten after another god: their drink offerings of blood will I not offer, nor take up their names into my lips.

⁵ The LORD is the portion of mine inheritance and of my cup: thou maintainest my lot.

⁶ The lines are fallen unto me in pleasant places; yea, I have a goodly heritage.

⁷ I will bless the LORD, who hath given me counsel: my reins also instruct me in the night seasons.

⁸ I have set the LORD always before me: because he is at my right hand, I shall not be moved.

⁹ Therefore my heart is glad, and my glory rejoiceth: my flesh also shall rest in hope.

¹⁰ For thou wilt not leave my soul in hell; neither wilt thou suffer thine Holy One to see corruption.

¹¹ Thou wilt shew me the path of life: in thy presence is fulness of joy; at thy right hand there are pleasures for evermore.

PURPOSES:

(i) Rejection of all forms of idolatry

(ii) Praying a prayer of confidence

(iii) Joy in god's presence

Here in Psalm sixteen, David in distrust of merit and man, fled to God for protection and preservation. In verse 2, he stresses his confidence in God by acknowledging God as his "LORD" and that he has no good beyond HIM (God). Hence he said, *"O my soul, thou hast said unto the LORD, Thou art my Lord, my goodness extended not to thee"*. Apart from God, David sees no meaning in his life and no personal happiness. Nothing in his life is good and joyful Paul expressed this same truth, when he said, "for to me to live is Christ". (*Philippians 1:21; Galatians 2:20*).

David categorically stated the consequence or reward of those whose "hasten" (go or run after) other gods or graven images forsaking God almighty as multiple sorrows, misery and adversities await them.

In verse 5, the psalmist ascertains his confidence in God and his possession of God's inheritance; David said, "The LORD is the portion of mine inheritance and my cup". What about you? What heritage do you have?

The "inheritance" and "cup" is the Lord Himself (*Psalms 73:26; Numbers 18:20; Deuteronomy 18:2*). An important aspect of our inheritance as New Testament believers is seen in the following: *"If a man loves me, he will keep my word and, my father will love him, and we will come unto him and make our abode with him"* (*John 14:23*).

Communion with God is the sure source of blessings and happiness.

For this goodly heritage, David glorified God, appreciated His divine counsel and he (David) in return meditate in the mighty and also maintained divine nearness to God.

He said, "I have set the LORD before me". This strengthened him the more, made him glad and gave him eternal hope.

Where do you find your joy and hope?

Believers should seek and cherish above all- intimate fellowship with God. The Lord's continued presence at our right hand brings His (God's) counsel (verse 7), protection (verse 8), joy (verse 9), resurrection (verse 10), and eternal blessings (verse 11).

David also expressed his certainty of God's assured security over his abandonment and death. He says, *"thou with not leave my soul in hell"* (verse 10). "Hell" here means the grave. A personal relationship with God will give believers confidence in a future life with God and the certainty that HE will not abandon them to the grave. (The Apostles Paul and Peter both applied this verse to Christ and His resurrection. (See *Acts 2:25-31; 13:34-37*).

David, the Psalmist, relied on God's divine guidance on the right path in his life as he enjoyed divine presence that enhances fullness of joy and pleasures till eternity. He had become an immovable saint.

What great TRUST, CONFIDENCE and goodly heritage indeed!

PUT YOUR TRUST IN GOD AND NOT MAN, EMULATE DAVID THE PSALMIST

PRAYER: God strengthen me to confirm my trust in you and to look unto thee only for protection preservation, provision and guidance all my life through. Give me the grace to enjoy your divine presence and your fullness of joy in all that I do in Jesus' name. Amen.

CHAPTER SEVENTEEN
EFFECTIVE PRAYER SATISFIED

BIBLE READING: PSALM 17 (King James Version)

Hear the right, O L<small>ORD</small>, attend unto my cry, give ear unto my prayer, that goeth not out of feigned lips.

² Let my sentence come forth from thy presence; let thine eyes behold the things that are equal.

³ Thou hast proved mine heart; thou hast visited me in the night; thou hast tried me, and shalt find nothing; I am purposed that my mouth shall not transgress.

⁴ Concerning the works of men, by the word of thy lips I have kept me from the paths of the destroyer.

⁵ Hold up my goings in thy paths, that my footsteps slip not.

⁶ I have called upon thee, for thou wilt hear me, O God: incline thine ear unto me, and hear my speech.

⁷ Shew thy marvellous lovingkindness, O thou that savest by thy right hand them which put their trust in thee from those that rise up against them.

⁸ Keep me as the apple of the eye, hide me under the shadow of thy wings,

⁹ From the wicked that oppress me, from my deadly enemies, who compass me about.

¹⁰ They are inclosed in their own fat: with their mouth they speak proudly.

¹¹ They have now compassed us in our steps: they have set their eyes bowing down to the earth;

¹² Like as a lion that is greedy of his prey, and as it were a young lion lurking in secret places.

¹³ Arise, O Lord, disappoint him, cast him down: deliver my soul from the wicked, which is thy sword:

¹⁴ From men which are thy hand, O Lord, from men of the world, which have their portion in this life, and whose belly thou fillest with thy hid treasure: they are full of children, and leave the rest of their substance to their babes.

¹⁵ As for me, I will behold thy face in righteousness: I shall be satisfied, when I awake, with thy likeness.

PURPOSE: Deliverance from the wicked

David cried to the LORD to hear his prayer based not only on God's mercy and grace but also on his faithful obedience to God's will and ways.

He presents his credentials of uprightness (*verses 1 to 5*); this serves as reasons why God must answer his prayers. He (David) then petitioned the LORD for protection from the wicked people in view of his hope for a better future (*verses 5 and 15*); with utmost trust and confidence (see *verses 6 and 7*).

David believed and trusted God alone could keep, hide and deliver him (see *verses 8 and 13)*. Such a great confidence in God is a good example for us. Let us no longer be afraid even if our enemies are doing what is stated in verse 9 -12. God knows how and when to defeat our enemies and satisfy us. Those who think, plan and carry-out evil against others, shall have the serious reward in verse 14. Therefore be warned.

God had searched David's heart and found that his endeavor to please him was no pretence. (See *I John 3:18-20*).

That David appealed to God on the basis of his own personal faithfulness expressed the fundamental truth that God had promised to hear the prayers of those who love and honor HIM (*John 15:1*).

The first indispensable condition of true prayer is a clear conscience and a pure life (*I John 3:22*) which invariably leads to effective prayers.

In verse 8, The Psalmists uses two figures of speech that recalls God's love and care for His faithful people;.

    i.   "*Keep me as the apple of the eye*", the apple of the eye is the pupil and a Hebrew metaphor expressing something greatly valued and dear.

    ii.   "*Hide me under the shadow of thy wings*". The shadow of thy wings is a metaphor drawn from the imagery of a hen protecting her young with her wings; thus it expresses tender protection. (*Psalm 51:1; 61:4; 63::7*).

    Christ used this metaphor to express his love for Israel. (*Matt. 23:37*)

WISDOM BOX:
   a. Contrast the in-ward character, the sins and the actions of David and his enemies, as revealed in this Psalm.
   b. In what ways do you resemble David and in what ways do you also resemble his enemies?

PRAYER: All believers should pray that God will reach out to protect us in times of danger just like someone who instinctively reacts to guard the pupil of the eye from harm (See *Deuteronomy 32:10; Proverbs 7:2; Zechariah 2:8*).

Also pray that the heavenly father will always be ready to hide and shield us as a mother-hen covers her chicks away from vultures (*Psalm 91:4; Matthew 23:37*).

Lord Jesus, I am precious to you, please keep me walking in the Holy Spirit.

Keep me steady in your ways, O! LORD, that I may not fall or go astray.

The believers and faithful should say and mean the prayers in *Luke 23:34; Acts 7:60*.

CHAPTER EIGHTEEN
THE RIGHTEOUSNESS OF GOD IN RELATION TO MAN'S LOYALTY

BIBLE READING: **PSALM 18 (King James Version)**

I will love thee, O LORD, my strength.

² The LORD is my rock, and my fortress, and my deliverer; my God, my strength, in whom I will trust; my buckler, and the horn of my salvation, and my high tower.

³ I will call upon the LORD, who is worthy to be praised: so shall I be saved from mine enemies.

⁴ The sorrows of death compassed me, and the floods of ungodly men made me afraid.

⁵ The sorrows of hell compassed me about: the snares of death prevented me.

⁶ In my distress I called upon the LORD, and cried unto my God: he heard my voice out of his temple, and my cry came before him, even into his ears.

⁷ Then the earth shook and trembled; the foundations also of the hills moved and were shaken, because he was wroth.

⁸ There went up a smoke out of his nostrils, and fire out of his mouth devoured: coals were kindled by it.

⁹ He bowed the heavens also, and came down: and darkness was under his feet.

¹⁰ And he rode upon a cherub, and did fly: yea, he did fly upon the wings of the wind.

¹¹ He made darkness his secret place; his pavilion round about him were dark waters and thick clouds of the skies.

¹² At the brightness that was before him his thick clouds passed, hail stones and coals of fire.

¹³ The LORD also thundered in the heavens, and the Highest gave his voice; hail stones and coals of fire.

¹⁴ Yea, he sent out his arrows, and scattered them; and he shot out lightnings, and discomfited them.

¹⁵ Then the channels of waters were seen, and the foundations of the world were discovered at thy rebuke, O LORD, at the blast of the breath of thy nostrils.

¹⁶ He sent from above, he took me, he drew me out of many waters.

¹⁷ He delivered me from my strong enemy, and from them which hated me: for they were too strong for me.

¹⁸ They prevented me in the day of my calamity: but the LORD was my stay.

¹⁹ He brought me forth also into a large place; he delivered me, because he delighted in me.

20 The LORD rewarded me according to my righteousness; according to the cleanness of my hands hath he recompensed me.

21 For I have kept the ways of the LORD, and have not wickedly departed from my God.

22 For all his judgments were before me, and I did not put away his statutes from me.

23 I was also upright before him, and I kept myself from mine iniquity.

24 Therefore hath the LORD recompensed me according to my righteousness, according to the cleanness of my hands in his eyesight.

25 With the merciful thou wilt shew thyself merciful; with an upright man thou wilt shew thyself upright;

26 With the pure thou wilt shew thyself pure; and with the froward thou wilt shew thyself froward.

27 For thou wilt save the afflicted people; but wilt bring down high looks.

28 For thou wilt light my candle: the LORD my God will enlighten my darkness.

29 For by thee I have run through a troop; and by my God have I leaped over a wall.

30 As for God, his way is perfect: the word of the LORD is tried: he is a buckler to all those that trust in him.

³¹ *For who is God save the* LORD? *or who is a rock save our God?*

³² *It is God that girdeth me with strength, and maketh my way perfect.*

³³ *He maketh my feet like hinds' feet, and setteth me upon my high places.*

³⁴ *He teacheth my hands to war, so that a bow of steel is broken by mine arms.*

³⁵ *Thou hast also given me the shield of thy salvation: and thy right hand hath holden me up, and thy gentleness hath made me great.*

³⁶ *Thou hast enlarged my steps under me, that my feet did not slip.*

³⁷ *I have pursued mine enemies, and overtaken them: neither did I turn again till they were consumed.*

³⁸ *I have wounded them that they were not able to rise: they are fallen under my feet.*

³⁹ *For thou hast girded me with strength unto the battle: thou hast subdued under me those that rose up against me.*

⁴⁰ *Thou hast also given me the necks of mine enemies; that I might destroy them that hate me.*

⁴¹ *They cried, but there was none to save them: even unto the* LORD, *but he answered them not.*

⁴² *Then did I beat them small as the dust before the wind: I did cast them out as the dirt in the streets.*

⁴³ *Thou hast delivered me from the strivings of the people; and thou hast made me the head of the heathen: a people whom I have not known shall serve me.*

⁴⁴ *As soon as they hear of me, they shall obey me: the strangers shall submit themselves unto me.*

⁴⁵ *The strangers shall fade away, and be afraid out of their close places.*

⁴⁶ *The LORD liveth; and blessed be my rock; and let the God of my salvation be exalted.*

⁴⁷ *It is God that avengeth me, and subdueth the people under me.*

⁴⁸ *He delivereth me from mine enemies: yea, thou liftest me up above those that rise up against me: thou hast delivered me from the violent man.*

⁴⁹ *Therefore will I give thanks unto thee, O LORD, among the heathen, and sing praises unto thy name.*

⁵⁰ *Great deliverance giveth he to his king; and sheweth mercy to his anointed, to David, and to his seed for evermore.*

PURPOSE: Royal thanksgiving.

Psalm 18 with fifty verses is the fourth longest in the Psalter and is found in II Samuel, chapter 22 with few changes. This psalm with the beginning "*I love thee O! LORD …………..*" was written after the death of Saul and was sang by David, the servant of God to the LORD when the LORD God delivered him from the hand of all his enemies and also for the securing of David's kingdom.

Thus, it commemorates David's overall deliverance from all his enemies rather than a specific victory writes Dr. Ryrie.

Psalm 18 can be categorized into two:

    i.   Verses 1 to 30 as an individual lament

    ii.   Verses 31 to 50 as a royal thanksgiving.

Note: II Samuel, Chapter 22 is the same as Psalm 18 – both are one royal thanksgiving.

The structure reveals an inclusionary motif (theme) around the praise of and the confidence in God, (Yahweh) the ROCK of Israel and the God of David. Whenever His servant is in need, the LORD swoops to deliver him, because He is just to those who love him (*verses 20 to 29*).

The focus of the text is the righteousness of God (verses 1 and 2; 46 to 50) in relation to David's loyalty (*verses 20-29*).

The structural divisions of the Psalm are as follows:
   a. Yahweh, the Rock of Israel (*verses 1 to 3*)
   b. Affliction (*verses 4 to 6*)
   c. The Lord's coming to help (*verses 7 to 15*)
   d. The Lord's deliverance (*verses 16 to19*)
   e. God's faithfulness to the faithful (*verses 20 to 29*)
   f. The divine perfection (*verses 30 to 36*)
   g. The kings' victory over the enemies (*verses 37 to 42*)
   h. The Glorious deliverance (*verses 43 to 45*)
   i. Yahweh the Rock of Israel (*verses 46 to 50*).

The Psalmist may speak prophetically of Christ; for Paul (the Apostle) quotes verse 49 as prophesying a time when through the messiah all nations will praise the name of God. (*Roman 15:9*).

David began this psalm by expressing his love for the Lord. To him, God was a rock" 'fortress', 'shield', and deliverer. He continued to describe God as "my God and my strength, in whom I will trust, my buckler and the horn of my salvation and my high tower" (verse 2)

The metaphors of this verse can be to the believers' perpetual struggles against physical and spiritual forces of this time (age).

God's care for us is described by six symbols which are:

i. **"My Rock"** - safety and security in God's immovable strength (see *Psalms 3:2-3; 42:9; 62:7*).

ii. **"My Fortress"** - a place of refuge and safety where the enemy cannot penetrate.

iii. **"My Deliverer"** - a living protector.

iv. **"My Buckler"** – a buckler is a type of shield, symbolizing that God comes between us and any form of harm. (see *Genesis 15:11*).

v. **"The Horn of my Salvation"** – strength and victorious power to deliver and save us.

vi. **"My High Tower"** – high place among the rocks safe from plunder and destruction.

- What are the equivalent defense and securities in which men trust today? Money, Fellow man, Position, Rank, Wealth and the likes.
- Is God to you all that these can give and more? Study *Habakkuk 3:17, 18, Hebrews 13:5-6*.

ANALYSIS OF PSALM 18 (THE ROYAL THANKSGIVING)

A. Part 1 (*Psalm 18:1-6*)

God allows problems and difficulties to come our way to make us:

- know who God really is (*verse 2*)
- believe that God is greater than our problems or enemies (*verses 2 and 3*)
- love and praise GOD ALWAYS (*verses 1 and 3*).
- know that such problems and difficulties we encounter are real, true, and part of life (*verses 4 and 5*)
- pray to God for help (*verses 3 and 6*)
- see our weakness and need of God in our daily living. (*verse 6*)
- Convinced that God hears and answers our prayers (*verse 6*).

B. PSALM 18:7-15

Here, we can see that God's anger and judgment against evil and sin are very serious indeed.

These verses 7 to 15 confirm Hebrews 10:31, which say *"it is a fearful thing to fall into the hands of the living God"*.

Psalm 18:15 also shows that your secret activities will soon be exposed by God. You are warned to stop playing pranks of sin with God, disobeying and dishonoring HIM. Sin is dangerous!

C. **Psalm 18:16-24.**

As we have read in verses16 to19, our confidence is that God answers prayers. His answer is best, surest and most timely. His (God) protection and deliverance are enough and complete. Verses 20-24 categorically tell us that God also rightly rewards us according to our deeds. No one that serves him faithfully will be disappointed. Faithful believers should be able to give such testimonies given by David in verses 20 to 24.

D. **PSALM 18:25-30**

What is God's will for man as to receive maximum blessing? God's will is that each of us should be loyal, merciful, blameless, pure and humble. This is the way to receive maximum blessings from HIM. God cannot tolerate pride in anybody (see *verse 27, Proverbs 8:1b*). Also James 1:17 and I John 15 states the reasons.

May God Almighty destroy all forms of pride in our heart and life in Jesus name. Amen.

Seven 7 other important facts contained in verses 28 to 30 about God. (Study and turn these verses into prayers).

- God will light my candle
- The LORD my God will enlighten my darkness
- For by thee (GOD) I have run through a troop by my God I have leaped over a wall.
- As for God, His way is perfect.
- The word of the Lord is tried.
- He is a bucker to all those that trust in him.

PRAYER: Turn verse 28 to 30 and the seven important facts above into prayer.

E. PSALM 18:31-36

The Christian race is difficult to run because there are spiritual enemies on the way and several wars to fight to be victorious; we must cling unto God as David did. God loves us and wants us to succeed and be in heaven with HIM, which is why HE gives us strength and guaranteed safety in our ways (verses 33-36).

Surely, our God is the LORD, a Rock that crushes and cannot be crushed. He is dependable and cannot be frightened. He is a trainer, supporter, strength, security and helper. Thank you God! For you are always there for me!.

F. PSALM 18:37-45

David achieved much and was very successful (see *verses 37and 38, 42 and 43*). This is a good example for us to emulate. Why? See John 15:5b; Philippians 4:13.

What are your achievements and successes? Are they the source of pride or praise to God for you? Verse 41 also spells out a hard but true fact for us that; those who neither honored, nor obeyed or prayed to God when all was well should not expect God's help when they are in trouble.

G. PSALM 18:46-50

From verses 1 to 45, we have read and seen the need to pray to God and trust HIM for his sure, best and timely unwavering answer. Here, verses 46 to 50 further teaches us that we need to praise Him for His numerous blessings for us every day. Verse 46 says, The Lord lives-this means HE was not only the God of the past years, but also our reliable and faithful God of the present time and of the future.

Let us pray to HIM, trust HIM, and praise HIM every day, every time, ever second, minute and hour.

HE (God) is available to bless us and be praised by us (His creation). Verse 49 is referred to Christ in Romans 15:19 as earlier said in the introduction.

Does this mean that the whole psalm can be taken as being in some way prophetic of Christ? If so, to what does it draw attention? Remember, The Lord lives; blessed be my Rock!

PRAYER: Lord, destroy very fiercely every form of evil in my life in Jesus name. Thank you God for being my source of strength, trainer, supporter, security and helper.

God, as you are alive through all generations, give me and my descendants the grace to praise and worship you always for you are a **GREAT FATHER**.

CHAPTER NINETEEN
GOD'S PERFECTION REVEALED IN HIS WORDS AND WORKS

BIBLE READING: PSALM 19 (King James Version)

The heavens declare the glory of God; and the firmament sheweth his handywork.

² Day unto day uttereth speech, and night unto night sheweth knowledge.

³ There is no speech nor language, where their voice is not heard.

⁴ Their line is gone out through all the earth, and their words to the end of the world. In them hath he set a tabernacle for the sun,

⁵ Which is as a bridegroom coming out of his chamber, and rejoiceth as a strong man to run a race.

⁶ His going forth is from the end of the heaven, and his circuit unto the ends of it: and there is nothing hid from the heat thereof.

⁷ The law of the LORD is perfect, converting the soul: the testimony of the LORD is sure, making wise the simple.

⁸ The statutes of the LORD are right, rejoicing the heart: the commandment of the LORD is pure, enlightening the eyes.

⁹ The fear of the LORD is clean, enduring for ever: the judgments of the LORD are true and righteous altogether.

¹⁰ *More to be desired are they than gold, yea, than much fine gold: sweeter also than honey and the honeycomb.*

¹¹ *Moreover by them is thy servant warned: and in keeping of them there is great reward.*

¹² *Who can understand his errors? cleanse thou me from secret faults.*

¹³ *Keep back thy servant also from presumptuous sins; let them not have dominion over me: then shall I be upright, and I shall be innocent from the great transgression.*

¹⁴ *Let the words of my mouth, and the meditation of my heart, be acceptable in thy sight, O LORD, my strength, and my redeemer.*

PURPOSE: For God's glory and wisdom in man's life

Psalm 19 can be subdivided into three structural components, which are:

A. Creation praise: The revelation of creation (verses 1 to 6).

B. A Wisdom psalm: The revelation of the law (verses 7 to 11).

C. A prayer of forgiveness and acceptance: The Prayerful reflection.

THE REVELATION OF CREATION (CREATION PRAISE) (Verses 1 to 6)

The psalmist considers the revelation of God in the world of nature. For him (David), creation reveals the Lord's royal majesty and sovereignty (*Romans 1:19-20*). It evokes a response of recognition of God's existence, majesty and wisdom and therefore of praise (*Romans 10:18*).

The hymn of creation praise is composed of two parts:
i. The revelation of the SKIES and
ii. The revelation of the SUN, MOON and STARS (*verses 4 to 6*).

The revelation of the skies (verse 1); the glory and wisdom of God are evident in the vastness of space. The psalmist calls attention to the word '*The Heavens*' as he begins the first verse, and concludes with the synonym '*The Skies*'

"The heavens ……….the Skies", signifies the place where God puts the sun, moon and stars for the purpose of giving light and for distinguishing 'day' from 'night' (*Genesis 1:14-19*).

For the psalmist (David), "space" is not empty but a revelation of God's creation of the magnificent heavenly bodies which are characterized by radiance and regularity.

While the "Heaven" and "Skies" keep on proclaiming the glory of God; the wars and disturbances on 'earth' often camouflage God's glory as they divert attention away from the created heavenly bodies which show more clearly God's majesty by their regularity and orderliness. God alone is the creator, because the magnificence of heavenly bodies confirm that they are all the works of his (God's) hands (See *Deuteronomy 4:19; 17:3*).

The alternation of 'Day' and 'night' reveals the constancy of God's creation (verse 2) "*day after day ……….. night after night*". The cycle of day and night contributes to the regularity of the seasons and thus to the regularity of the agricultural calendar (*Genesis 8:22*).

"They display knowledge" (*verse 2*) means they revealed the "knowledge" in their own distinct 'speech'. The 'knowledge' is not only about God but rather about a special kind best understood as God's wisdom, reveals in His creation (*Proverbs 8:22-31*).

Natural revelation is without words (verse 3) (.... "*there is no speech or language ....*") and is universal, being unrestricted by the division of languages. It transcends human communication without the use of speech, words and sounds. To those who are inclined to hear, revelation comes with no regard for linguistics or geographical barriers, even to the ends of the world (verse 4).

The revelation of the sun; life on earth depends on the regularity of the sun. The Psalmist (David) did not have the knowledge of today's solar system but his interest was to portray in a phenomenal way, how the sun rises as it were from a 'tent' (verse 4c).

The tabernacle is metaphorically compared to a "bridegroom" and to a "champion" (verse 5). The joy of the bridegroom coming from the wedding canopy or the bridal chamber, represents the radiance of the sun. The "champion" (a warrior, valiant or winner of a competition) rejoicing in his strength as he sets out to run his course, represents the power of the SUN, as it seems to move through its 'circuit" with radiance and vigor in order to warm the earth.

The sun like the heavens and skies also reveals God's glory, power and wisdom. One does not have to listen to words or language as the effect of the SUN is evident as nothing is hidden from its heat.

THE REVELATION OF THE LAW–A WISDOM PSALM (Verses 7 to 11)

After describing the skies as a reflection of God's glory in the first six verses, Psalm 19 switches gear from the heavenly bodies (sun, stars, moons) and turns to consider the beauty of GOD'S LAW.

Here, the poem in Hebrew uses a different, more personal name for God. The first six verses refer to God with a general name that anyone of any religion, might use - just like our English word 'God'. But from verse seven on, God is called "the Lord" (a translation of Hebrew – YAHWEH); the personal name God revealed to Moses from the burning bush. (*Exodus 3:15*). *"The heavens declare the glory of God"*, but God's law reveals even more - his personal voice to his chosen people. He introduces himself to the world by his first name as it were.

"The law of the LORD is perfect" tells us the revelation of God's law is clearer (verses 7 to 11). God's creation ("declares", proclaims' "pours forth") and displays God's majesty, wisdom and power, while the revelation of the law is greater as it is given by the covenant God whose name is YAHWEH - "Lord" (*verses 7,8,9*). Nature, which is God's creation, also reveals the glory of God.

These verses 7 to 11 speak of five facets of this greater revelation.

i. **"The law"** – This reflects the moral character of God, and is thus "perfect" in its life giving influence on the soul. (*verse 7*)

ii. **"The testimony"** – This represents God's wisdom and will that are "trustworthy" for making wise and prudent decisions in life. (verse 7)

iii. **"The statutes"** – This comprises of God's principles for right living, that produce the "joy" of being alive and receiving his blessings. (verse 8)

iv. **"The commandments of the Lord"** – This radiates God's light, thereby "enlightening the eyes" (verse 8) for living righteous in consonant relationships and in the wholesome "fear of the Lord" with enduring results (verse 9).

v. **"The judgments"** – These are laws governing social life that insure justice and righteous treatment for the whole covenant community (verse 9) being more desired or valuable than gold (verse 10).

Benefits of Embracing God's Law

All the words of the Lord are beneficial, although the benefits of God's creation which are natural revelations are with us on a daily basis.

To encourage the godly to embrace the law of God as an expression of his wisdom, are given to us four benefits. It is worthy to note that the rewards of good and prompt response to the revelation of God are compared to gold (*Psalm 19:10; Proverbs 3:13-18; 8:19*) and to honey (*Proverbs 16:24*).

The four benefits are set forth propositionally (verses 7 to 9).

    i.   Firstly, God's words revive. (verse 7) Its' restorative quality gives healing to the whole person by assuring forgiveness and cleansing and by giving life to the godly. It unleashes the promise of God by His gracious redemptive acts. (*Psalm 80:3, 7, 19*).

    ii.   Secondly, God's word is the source of wisdom to all who are ready to receive it (*Psalm 19:7; Psalm 119:130; Proverbs 21:11*) Both the inexperienced or the simple (*verse 7; Proverbs 1:4*) and the wise develop as they begin with the fear of the Lord (*verse 9; Deuteronomy 4:10; Proverbs 1:7*) and embrace the will of God in all aspects of life (*Proverbs 1: 2-6*).

    iii.   Thirdly, God's word gives joy (*verse 8a*). The heartfelt joy is equivalent to inner peace and tranquility as one loves God with all his heart and innermost being.

iv. Finally, God's word gives light to the eyes (verse 8b).The internal joy radiates through the "eyes". It expresses the joy of being alive and receiving God's blessings (*Psalm 13:3*). Thus YAHWEH (LORD) has made the sun for light in creation and has given his word for light in redemption.

THE SUPERIORITY OF GOD'S LAW OVER GOD'S CREATION (THE NATURE)

The reason why the revelation of God in his word is superior to natural (God's creation) revelation lies in its clarity and openness to all. God's written revelation manifests a perfect internal harmony between God and His word.

God's word reflects His integrity, uprightness, and fidelity - *blameless* (*Psalm 18:25*). God's words are trustworthy in the sense that His statutes are true in principle and are verifiable in every situation of life (*Psalm 93:5; 111:7*). It is "right" in the sense of been straight forward and just. God's word is not perverse or crooked but encourages the godly to be upright. It is enduring forever (*verse 9*) as it does not change with the times and the incessant variations of fashion. God's word (law) is always "in". It is sure (verse 9), faithful and true (*Psalm119:151,160*) as it reflects the fidelity and loyalty of God. It has in itself revelatory qualities and has transforming effects on the godly.

It is therefore of greater value than the most valuable objects of man's striving – money and gold (*Ps 119:72*) and fine food (*verse 10; Psalm 119:103*).

The law of God keeps the wise man on the narrow path by fore - warning him of possible pitfalls (*verse 11a*) and by guiding him onto the rewards of a godliness kind of life, God given joy, wisdom and contentment (*verses 7 to 9; Proverbs 22:4; I Timothy 4:8; 6:6*). It is radiant, that is, pure, and its purity affects the clean and upright way of those who are "pure" (see *Psalm 18:26*).

THE PRAYERFUL REFLECTION: A PRAYER OF FORGIVENESS AND ACCEPTANCE: (PSALM 19:12 to 14)

In psalm 8, when David (the Psalmist) reflected on God's glory in the heaven he had his focus on man, looking at his (man) dignity (*Psalm 8:4a*).

Here in Psalm 19, the Psalmist reflected on himself in relation to God and his revelations. God is perfect and his revelation in nature and word reveals His glory, power and wisdom; but man is such an in- significant part of the vastness of space.

Just as nothing is hidden from the sun, (*verse 6*) and even as the voice of the natural revelation penetrates to the ends of the earth (verse 4), so does God's word with all its perfections penetrates and examines man (*verse 7 to 9*).

The godly man therefore stands in fear before his creator, redeemer; knowing that he may have "secret faults" or errors (*verse 12)* that he has not yet discovered.

Inadvertent sin had to be dealt with by the atonement of this sin (*Numbers 15: 22-31*). This had been done by Christ on the cross with his death (O.T). (*Psalm 19:12 - …"Cleanse thou me from "secret faults"… *).

Here David (the Psalmist) showed even a conscientiousness pertaining to the "secret faults" because he aimed at pleasing God so as to live blameless and upright before God. (See *Psalm 18:25b; Job 1:1, 4-5*). Therefore he (David) asked for forgiveness and an ability to express humility and contrition. He desired true godliness according to which he will not knowingly sin against his God - *"keep back thy servant also from presumptions sins; let them not have dominion over me" (verse 13)*.

Believers should endeavor to love and serve God with all their hearts (*Deuteronomy 6:5*) because they are still imperfect in this life. However, they may fall short of God's will without knowing it and thus need to seek God's forgiveness for their errors and "secret faults".

On the other hand, presumptions or willful sins are great transgressions (*verse 13*) that involve despising God, His word and the loss of a place in His kingdom (See *Numbers 15:30-31; Galatians 5:19-21*).

It should, however, be noted that the wicked sin in their arrogance and show no awareness of having done wrong. "Willful sins" are those often attributed to the arrogant, which have no regard for God.

In Psalm19 verse 14, the Psalmist closes with a prayer saying, "Let the words of my mouth and the meditation of my heart, be acceptable in thy sight, O Lord, my strength, and my redeemer". (See *Psalm 78:35; Exodus1:13; Isaiah 63:9*).

The proper response to the work of salvation in our lives is a constant prayer that God will keep our hearts, words and lives free from sin and pleasing to HIM. Both the meditation of our hearts and the reflection of our minds should be acceptable to God. Amen.

FACTS TO LIVE WITH FROM PSALM 19

1. The Law (Torah) in a broad sense refers to any "instruction" flowing from the revelation of God as the basis for life and action.
2. The Godly is receptive to commune with and practice the instructions of God. (*Psalm 40:8*).
3. God's revelation demarcates the way of God and the righteous person delights in staying within its perimeters (*Psalm 19:7a*).

4. The LAW of his God is heart, feet, does not slip, (*Psalm 37:31; 40:8; Jeremiah 3:33*).
5. The expression of internalization is 'delight in God's revelation' (*Psalm 1:2; 119:70, 77,113,163 and 174*).
6. The psalmist exalts divine speech as everything that proceeds from the mouth of the LORD.

PRAYER: Make verses 12, 13, 14 and Psalm 119:77 your prayer points.

Ps. 19:12 - "cleanse *thou me from secret faults*".

Ps19:13 - "*keep back thy servant also from presumptuous sins; let them not have dominion over me*"..........

Ps. 19:14- "*Let the words of my mouth and the meditation of my heart, be acceptable in thy sight..........*"

Ps.119:77 - "*Let thy tender mercies come unto me, that I may live for thy law is my delight*".

CHAPTER TWENTY
PRAYER FOR VICTORY

BIBLE READING: PSALM 20 (King James Version)

The LORD hear thee in the day of trouble; the name of the God of Jacob defend thee;

² Send thee help from the sanctuary, and strengthen thee out of Zion;

³ Remember all thy offerings, and accept thy burnt sacrifice; Selah.

⁴ Grant thee according to thine own heart, and fulfil all thy counsel.

⁵ We will rejoice in thy salvation, and in the name of our God we will set up our banners: the LORD fulfil all thy petitions.

⁶ Now know I that the LORD saveth his anointed; he will hear him from his holy heaven with the saving strength of his right hand.

⁷ Some trust in chariots, and some in horses: but we will remember the name of the LORD our God.

⁸ They are brought down and fallen: but we are risen, and stand upright.

⁹ Save, LORD: let the king hear us when we call.

PURPOSE: For Life's Battle

Psalms twenty and twenty-one are companion psalms. They are prayers to God before battle.

For us believers in Christ, Psalm 20 can be a applied to our spiritual warfare. The Psalm begins thus *"The Lord hear thee in the day of trouble ……"*.
We now struggle against unseen, yet very real forces of evil and we yearn over and wants deliverance from Satan and demonic powers (*Ephesians 6:12*).

Here in this psalm, the church blesses the king in his exploits. She expresses a confidence in God's favor asking for divine protection, help and support.

PRAYER: God! My father let me be favored by you mightily and bless me abundantly with divine providence, protection, loving kindness, constant grace and support throughout my life's pilgrimage in Jesus' name. Amen.

May I be victorious in all my life's battle to your glory in Jesus mighty name I pray. Amen.

CHAPTER TWENTY - ONE
SPLENDOR AND SUCCESS OF THE KING

BIBLE READING: **PSALM 21 (King James Version)**

The king shall joy in thy strength, O LORD; and in thy salvation how greatly shall he rejoice!

² Thou hast given him his heart's desire, and hast not withholden the request of his lips. Selah.

³ For thou preventest him with the blessings of goodness: thou settest a crown of pure gold on his head.

⁴ He asked life of thee, and thou gavest it him, even length of days for ever and ever.

⁵ His glory is great in thy salvation: honour and majesty hast thou laid upon him.

⁶ For thou hast made him most blessed for ever: thou hast made him exceeding glad with thy countenance.

⁷ For the king trusteth in the LORD, and through the mercy of the most High he shall not be moved.

⁸ Thine hand shall find out all thine enemies: thy right hand shall find out those that hate thee.

⁹ *Thou shalt make them as a fiery oven in the time of thine anger: the LORD shall swallow them up in his wrath, and the fire shall devour them.*

¹⁰ *Their fruit shalt thou destroy from the earth, and their seed from among the children of men.*

¹¹ *For they intended evil against thee: they imagined a mischievous device, which they are not able to perform.*

¹² *Therefore shalt thou make them turn their back, when thou shalt make ready thine arrows upon thy strings against the face of them.*

¹³ *Be thou exalted, LORD, in thine own strength: so will we sing and praise thy power.*

PURPOSE: Praising God over success OR Success / Praise for Victory

This Psalter comprises of two parts: (a) verses 1 to 7 and (b) verses 8 to 13.

Psalm 21: 1-7 is a song of praise sang by the Psalmist – David who rejoiced greatly and thanked God for giving him his heart's desire as king; giving him joy, long life, honor and majesty and for blessing him abundantly. He exalted God the Almighty (*verse 13*).

It is important for us to note that David's past, present and future blessings depended on God's help, strength, presence, and steadfast love as well as David's trust in God (*Verse 7*).

Has God done any special thing for you? How grateful are you to God? Remember to praise and thank God for his numerous victories, kindness, mercies, provisions, etc he has bestowed on you.

Show gratitude to Almighty God always. Let your praise and thanksgiving supersede your request from HIM.

Psalm 21:8-13 sees God's enemies as those who refuse to believe in prayer, praise, worship, and obey HIM. These are those who do not believe that Jesus Christ is the Son of God, savior and Lord. Those who have not allowed the Holy Spirit to control their thoughts, words and deeds (actions)

David believed that God had and still has the strength, power, wisdom and would deal seriously with such people and their children (verses 9 and 10) and their evil plans.

For expected and obtained victories praise God always! It is dangerous to be God's enemy. You are warned.

PRAYER: Father! Thank you for your steadfast love that never cease. You mercy never comes to an end; be exalted oh! LORD in your strength.

LORD, God! Have mercy; help your enemies to become your friends before it is too late for them.

CHAPTER TWENTY - TWO
A CRY OF ANGUISH AND A SONG OF THE CROSS

BIBLE READING: PSALM 22 (King James Version)

My God, my God, why hast thou forsaken me? why art thou so far from helping me, and from the words of my roaring?

² O my God, I cry in the day time, but thou hearest not; and in the night season, and am not silent.

³ But thou art holy, O thou that inhabitest the praises of Israel.

⁴ Our fathers trusted in thee: they trusted, and thou didst deliver them.

⁵ They cried unto thee, and were delivered: they trusted in thee, and were not confounded.

⁶ But I am a worm, and no man; a reproach of men, and despised of the people.

⁷ All they that see me laugh me to scorn: they shoot out the lip, they shake the head, saying,

⁸ He trusted on the LORD that he would deliver him: let him deliver him, seeing he delighted in him.

⁹ But thou art he that took me out of the womb: thou didst make me hope when I was upon my mother's breasts.

¹⁰ *I was cast upon thee from the womb: thou art my God from my mother's belly.*

¹¹ *Be not far from me; for trouble is near; for there is none to help.*

¹² *Many bulls have compassed me: strong bulls of Bashan have beset me round.*

¹³ *They gaped upon me with their mouths, as a ravening and a roaring lion.*

¹⁴ *I am poured out like water, and all my bones are out of joint: my heart is like wax; it is melted in the midst of my bowels.*

¹⁵ *My strength is dried up like a potsherd; and my tongue cleaveth to my jaws; and thou hast brought me into the dust of death.*

¹⁶ *For dogs have compassed me: the assembly of the wicked have inclosed me: they pierced my hands and my feet.*

¹⁷ *I may tell all my bones: they look and stare upon me.*

¹⁸ *They part my garments among them, and cast lots upon my vesture.*

¹⁹ *But be not thou far from me, O LORD: O my strength, haste thee to help me.*

²⁰ *Deliver my soul from the sword; my darling from the power of the dog.*

²¹ *Save me from the lion's mouth: for thou hast heard me from the horns of the unicorns.*

²² I will declare thy name unto my brethren: in the midst of the congregation will I praise thee.

²³ Ye that fear the LORD, praise him; all ye the seed of Jacob, glorify him; and fear him, all ye the seed of Israel.

²⁴ For he hath not despised nor abhorred the affliction of the afflicted; neither hath he hid his face from him; but when he cried unto him, he heard.

²⁵ My praise shall be of thee in the great congregation: I will pay my vows before them that fear him.

²⁶ The meek shall eat and be satisfied: they shall praise the LORD that seek him: your heart shall live for ever.

²⁷ All the ends of the world shall remember and turn unto the LORD: and all the kindreds of the nations shall worship before thee.

²⁸ For the kingdom is the LORD's: and he is the governor among the nations.

²⁹ All they that be fat upon earth shall eat and worship: all they that go down to the dust shall bow before him: and none can keep alive his own soul.

³⁰ A seed shall serve him; it shall be accounted to the Lord for a generation.

³¹ They shall come, and shall declare his righteousness unto a people that shall be born, that he hath done this.

PURPOSE: In times of Trials and Sufferings

This Psalm can be divided into two parts as the title implies:

(a) A cry of anguish or agony (verses 1 to 21)

(b) A song of praise (verses 22 to 31).

This Psalm is the one of the most quoted in the New Testament and it is referred to or called "The song of the Cross" because it so precisely portrays Christ's anguished sufferings on the cross.

There are at least two facts about this Psalm which are:

1. It is a cry of anguish and grief from a godly sufferer who has not yet been delivered from trials and suffering. In this sense, all suffering believers can identify with the words of this prayer (read *Psalm 22*).

2. The words of the Psalm express an experience far beyond that of any ordinary human experience inspired by the Holy Spirit. The Psalmist both predicts the suffering of Jesus Christ in his crucifixion and points to his subsequent vindication three days later.

A Cry of Anguish or Agony (Verses 1 to 21)

Verse 1 – "*My God, my God, why hast thou forsaken me?*"

These words were uttered by Jesus Christ on the cross at the peak of this pain in suffering when He felt his Heavenly Father withdrew his Holy and intimate presence. (*Isaiah 53:4-6, 8, 10-12; II Corinthians 5:21, Mathew 27:46*).

Jesus was also claiming the entire psalm as a description of himself by quoting this Psalm.

Verse 2 - *"but thou hearesth not"*

The believer, like Jesus Himself may at times feel forsaken by God. When this occurs, hold fast to the revelation of God's love and goodness towards you; continue to pray and trust HIM. (*verse 2 to 5*).

In verse 7, the mockery is echoed by the priests. Matthew 27:39 states that *"they that passed by reviled him (Christ) wagging (shaking) their heads"*. The very gestures of Jesus' enemies were predicted in this Old Testament. Verse 8 states that the Psalmist like Jesus trusted in the LORD God.

The rest of the Psalm shows that although it was a genuine experience of the psalmist, it foreshadows the experience of Christ.

Verses 11 to 19 describe the exact feelings and helplessness of Jesus Christ while going through the brutality of the scourging and crucifixion.

Here we see the righteous suffering in the hands of the enemies, unlike in many other psalms, where there were no calls for vengeance (*Romans 12:17-19*).

Although the sufferings of the psalmist were heightened by God's apparent silence (*verse 1*), he was able to cry to the Lord. Why? See verses 4, 5, 9 to 11. *"Our fathers trusted in thee; they trusted and thou did deliver them. They cried unto thee……… "But thou art he that took me out of the womb; …..……….thou art my God from my mother's belly".*

Did these recollections of the past and of who God is (*verse 3*) help his (Psalmist) faith?

As we pass through great tribulations, our feelings often overwhelm us. We fail to see God working through these sufferings; though, God may appear distant and silent, He is there with us; He will never forsake his own.

The lament of the Psalmist continues in verses twelve through seventeen. In fact, this verse simply describes the Lord's feelings of helplessness while undergoing the brutality of the scourging and crucifixion. The experiences of the Psalmist in verses 14, 15 and 16a solidly tells of his agony while verses 12 and 13 describes what the enemies did to him, the actuaries, that of verse 16b to 18 are exactly the experiences and horrors Christ went through at crucifixion. ... *'they pierced my hands and my feet'... "thou look and stared upon me"... "they part my garments among them, and cast lots upon my vesture"* (*verses 16b to 18*) For further understanding, study *John 19:23-24; John 20:25; Mathew 27:35; Mark 15:24; Luke 23:34.*

The cry of deliverance unto God by the psalmist continues in verses 19 through to 21. This simply tells us that we must persistently continue in prayer for our request without being tired until God gives us an answer.

PRAYER: O! Lord, help me to always depend on your WORD and not my feelings (Psalm 22:11).

A Song of Praise (verses 22 to 31)

After darkness comes sunshine, so says an adage. Thank God that the psalmist in verses 22 to 31 exhibited praise after perplexity. This could come into reality because of his unwavering faith in God and an anticipated answer for the deliverance. Anybody who received God's favor, shares a personal testimony (verse 22), encourages others (verse 23) and promises to fulfill the vow he has made.

This verse 22 compared to Hebrew 2:11-12 relates to Jesus Christ triumph of the cross. He is now an exalted REDEEMER who gathers round HIM. Christ's death result in the help for the afflicted (*verse 24*), eternal life (*verse 26*). Only those who have experienced the love and deliverance of God can truly proclaim the full message of the Gospel (*verse 27*), His rule over all nations and ultimate exaltation and glory to others (*verses 30 and 31*).

Worthy is the lamb Jesus Christ; Call on HIM, wait upon HIM, HE will surely answer you!.

PRAYER: God my father, I thank you that weeping may endure for a night but joy cometh in the morning. I glorify you father for the assurance that if I sow in tears, I will reap in joy Amen.

God make those who do not know Christ, know HIM, the power of His resurrection and the fellowship of sharing in His suffering becoming like HIM in his death.

CHAPTER TWENTY - THREE
THE SHEPHERD'S PSALM – DAVID'S CONFIDENCE IN GOD'S GRACE

BIBLE READING: PSALM 23 (King James Version)

The LORD is my shepherd; I shall not want.

² He maketh me to lie down in green pastures: he leadeth me beside the still waters.

³ He restoreth my soul: he leadeth me in the paths of righteousness for his name's sake.

⁴ Yea, though I walk through the valley of the shadow of death, I will fear no evil: for thou art with me; thy rod and thy staff they comfort me.

⁵ Thou preparest a table before me in the presence of mine enemies: thou anointest my head with oil; my cup runneth over.

⁶ Surely goodness and mercy shall follow me all the days of my life: and I will dwell in the house of the LORD for ever.

PURPOSE: -For Divine Protection, Provision, Guidance and Restoration

David, the psalmist knows, recognizes and accepts God the LORD as his shepherd. This strong conviction of God as David's shepherd had positive effect on his thoughts about his present and his future.

What effect has the knowledge of God got on for you? Let us have a meaningful insight into the shepherd's Psalm. This Psalm (23) is the most popular of the psalms and the most easily memorized.

It celebrates the loving care of God. He is the 'Shepherd' who is all sufficient and is always at work on behalf of His people.

- This psalm conceived in the mind of the Lord and inspired by the Holy Spirit expresses His (God's) concern and diligent care for those who follow Him. They are cherished objects of His divine love. He cares for each of them as a father cares for his children and as a shepherd for his sheep. It should be noted that God's people are His sheep (*Psalm 74:1; 79:13; Matthew 10:16; 15:24; Isaiah 40:11; Zechariah 9:16*).

In this Psalm (23), there are "Seven Acts" of God's graces. They are:

1st Act of God's Grace

"The Lord is My Shepherd" - Here in this first act of God's grace, David God likens God to a shepherd in order to illustrate His great love for His people.(*Psalm 28:9; 79:13; 80:1; 95:7; Isaiah 40:11; Jeremiah 31:10*).

The Lord Jesus Himself adopted the same metaphor to express His relationship to His people (*John 10:11-16; Hebrews 13:20; I Peter 5:4; Revelation 7:17*).

Two facts are established and emphasized here:
   i. That God through Jesus Christ by the Holy Spirit is so concerned about each of His children that He desires to love, care for, protect, guide and be near them; just as a good shepherd does to his own sheep.
   ii. Believers are the Lord's sheep. We belong to Him and are the special objects of His affection and attention. Isaiah 40:11 says, *"He shall feed His flock like a shepherd; He shall gather the lambs*

with his arm, and carry them in his bosom, and shall gently lead those that are with his young". *(Isaiah 49:10; Ezekiel 34:23; 37:24; John 10:11; Hebrews 13:20; I peter 2:25; 5:4; Revelation 2:17).* This is absolute spiritual guidance. Though *"All we like sheep have gone astray"* (Isaiah 53:6). The Lord Jesus has redeemed us with His shed blood at Calvary (I Peter 1:18-19) and we now belong to HIM.

As His sheep, when we respond to HIS voice and follow Him, then we can claim the promises of this Psalm. (Read *John 10:3-5; John 10:28).*

2nd Act of God's Grace

"I shall not want". - "Not want" here could mean basically two things.

i. That I will not lack anything necessary for God's will to be accomplished in my life (*3 John 2*); spiritual food inclusive (*Isaiah 40:11*). I will be enriched by God with divine supplies in times of need. Spiritual abundance will not elude me – Abundant Grace (*II Corinthians 9:8*), Abundant Power (*Ephesians 3:2*), Abundant supplies

(*Philippians 4:19*), Abundant entrance (*II Peter 1:11*). I am confident in God's promise of plenty in the bible (*Leviticus 26:5; Deuteronomy 30:9; Psalm 132:15; Isaiah 30:23; Amos 9:13*).

ii. That I will be contented in the Good shepherd is provision and care for my life even in times of personal hardship because I trust in His love and His commitment to me. (*John 10:11, Philippians 4:11-13*).

3rd Act of God's Grace:

"*He maketh me to lie down*" - I can lie down in peace, free from all fears because of the presence and nearness of the '*Shepherd*'. The Holy Spirit as my comforter, counselor and helper communicates Christ's Shepherded care and presence to me (*John 14:16-18; II Timothy 1:7*).

My confidence resting in His presence will be experienced "***in green pastures***". That is, in Jesus and in the word of God, which are necessary for an abundant life. (*John 6:32-35; 63; 8:31; 10:9: and 15:7*).

Where He brings us (*"in green pasture and quiet waters"*) is a place of greater blessing and satisfaction where we will experience a higher level of righteousness. Every Christian can experience God's *"green pastures"* and "quiet waters" each day as he meets with Him in prayer and bible reading.(*Psalm 1:1-3*). What is your relationship with God like?

4th ACT of God's Grace
"He restoreth my soul"

When I become discouraged (*Psalm 42:11*), the Good shepherd' revives and re-energizes my soul through His power and grace (*Proverbs 25:13*). "He gives me complete restoration then as divine leader, He leads me through the right path. (*Proverbs 25:10; Psalm 31:3*).

How and where does God lead His people?

God leads His people:

  i. in difficult places for tests (*Deuteronomy 8:2*)
  ii. like a mother - bird teaching her young to fly (*Deuteronomy 32:11-12*).
  iii. in plain paths (*Psalm 27:11; Luke 24:50 - 51*)
  iv. like a shepherd (*Psalm 77:20*)

v. To no place beyond the reach of His hand (*Psalm 139:9-10, Proverbs 20:24; Isaiah 63:14*).

vi. steadily towards the cross (*Matthew 10:32*).

vii. to the border of the unseen.

God's Holy Spirit also guides me in His chosen path, the one that conform to His way of holiness which is the way of all truth. (*Romans 8:15-14; John 16:13; Acts 4*)

My response is obedience. I follow the shepherd and hear His voice. (*John 10:3-4*). I will not follow the voice of strangers (*John 10:5*).

5th Act of God's Grace

"Thou art with me"

In times of dangers, difficulties and even death, I fear no evil. Why? *"For thou art with me"*. In every situation of life (*Matthew 28:20)*, I have great confidence that God is present with me every time (*Psalm 27:3; Isaiah 12:2*). There is an undoubted fact and I am sure that God is my divine helper and friend. Hence, He is with me always (*John 15:15*).

Purpose of his divine presence

We need and experience His divine presence in the following ways:

i. in the pilgrimage of life (*Genesis 28:15*)
ii. it affords us rest (*Exodus 38:14; Leviticus 26:12*)
iii. it gives courage in life's battle (*Deuteronomy 20:1*)
iv. a comfort in times of trials (*Isaiah 43:2; Zechariah 2:10*)
v. assured to the smallest assembly of believers (*Matthew 18:20*)
vi. unto the end (*Matthew 28:20*)

"thy rod and thy staff they comfort me"

The '*rod*' (a short club) is a weapon of defense or discipline symbolizing God's strength, power and authority (*Exodus 21:20; Job. 9:34*).

The '*staff*' (a long slender stick with a hook on one end) is used to draw a sheep close to the shepherd, guide it in the right way or rescue it from trouble.

God's rod and staff reassures us of God's love and guidance in our lives *(Psalm 71:21; 86:17)*.

Again in everyday life, we have God's divine presence, protection and preparation in our life's journey. (*Psalm 31:19; 68:10; Isaiah 64:4*).

6th Act of God's Grace

"Thou preparest a table before me in the presence of my enemies"

God is here seen as caring for my needs in the midst of the forces of evil that attempt to destroy my life and soul (*Roman 8:31-39*).

Confronted daily by satan and surrounded by an ungodly society, I am furnished with sufficient GRACE to live and rejoice in God's presence. (*II Corinthians 12:9-10*).

Provided for me is God's (divine) spiritual feast prepared in abundance. (*Isaiah 25:6; Mark 14:22; Revelation 19:19*) I may eat at the Lord's Table in faith, thanksgiving and hope, fully at peace and protected by His shed blood and broken body of this Good shepherd - Jesus Christ (*I Corinthians 11:23; Mark 14:22*).

7th Act of God's Grace

"...anointest my head with oil"

The anointing of my head with oil by God refers to His (GOD) special favor and lavish blessing through the anointing of His Holy Spirit upon my body, mind and spirit (Ephesians 5:18). I am therefore flowing with:

i. Spiritual fullness which - blessed with overflowing cup (*Malachi 3:10*).

ii. Fullness of joy. (*John 15:11; Romans 15:29*)

iii. Fullness of God. (*Ephesians 3:19*)

iv. Fullness of the spirit. (*Ephesians 5:18*)

v. Fullness of Christ (*John 1:16; Ephesians 1:23; 4:13; Colossians 1:19*)

Man's response to God's Act of Grace - "*goodness & mercy shall follow me…..*"

Mercy means God's faithful love and kindness while goodness is the high quality of God's actions, behavior or probably the way He intervenes in my (our) affairs. With the "*Shepherd*" accompanying me (us) through life's pilgrimage, I will receive constant grace, help, kindness and support. I can trust the Good shepherd to work in all things together for my (our) good. (*Romans 8:28; James 5:11; Psalm 34:8; Nahum 1:7; Psalm 33:5*).

My Responsibility to the Good Shepherd

The goal of following the Good shepherd and experiencing His "goodness" and "mercy" is that I may be with the Lord forever. (*I Thessalonians 4:17; Psalm 27:4; Psalm 26:8*) see His face and serve Him forever in His house (*Revelation 22:3; John 14:2-3*).

The Psalm portrays the great confidence that the Psalmist had in God.

As we saw in Psalm 22, the fact that the Lord is leading, guiding, providing, and doing other things to and for us, does not prelude suffering in our lives. In the midst of whatever sufferings He allows, His presence is always a source of comfort and confidence. (verses 4-5).

FOR FURTHER STUDY

a. For kings as shepherd, study *II Samuel 5:2; Isaiah 44:28*.

b. For Jesus as a shepherd, study *John 10:11-14; Hebrews 13:20; 1 Peter 5:4.*

c. For Jesus as the Shepherd and King Study *Revelations*

d. For Leaders, Heads of Organizations, Institutions, Countries, Nations, Families as shepherd, study

e. A modern shepherd (*John 10:10,15*)

PRAYER: God our heavenly father, May the sheep who are harassed and helpless come to your shepherding care in Jesus' name. Amen.

CHAPTER TWENTY - FOUR
THE DIVINE OWNER CUM KING OF GLORY

BIBLE READING: PSALM 24 (King James Version)

The earth is the LORD's, and the fulness thereof; the world, and they that dwell therein.

² For he hath founded it upon the seas, and established it upon the floods.

³ Who shall ascend into the hill of the LORD? or who shall stand in his holy place?

⁴ He that hath clean hands, and a pure heart; who hath not lifted up his soul unto vanity, nor sworn deceitfully.

⁵ He shall receive the blessing from the LORD, and righteousness from the God of his salvation.

⁶ This is the generation of them that seek him, that seek thy face, O Jacob. Selah.

⁷ Lift up your heads, O ye gates; and be ye lift up, ye everlasting doors; and the King of glory shall come in.

⁸ Who is this King of glory? The LORD strong and mighty, the LORD mighty in battle.

⁹ *Lift up your heads, O ye gates; even lift them up, ye everlasting doors; and the King of glory shall come in.*

¹⁰ *Who is this King of glory? The LORD of hosts, he is the King of glory. Selah.*

PURPOSE: - Need for Purity and Sanctification

This Psalm might have been written at the time the 'Ark' was brought to Jerusalem (*II Samuel 6:12-19*). The victorious 'King of glory' who delivered the Israelites from Egypt and led them through the wilderness had a great reception into the Holy City. This Psalm 24 can be studied and is divided into three main parts for quick and easy understanding.

i. Creator - The divine owner
ii. Requirements for accessing God's kingdom
iii. Promises to the righteous that meets the requirements or set standards in this psalm.

Psalm 24:1- 2 talks about the creator as the divine owner of the earth, its fullness, the world and its entire inhabitants (*Isaiah 6:3*)

God emphasizes His ownership in Psalm 50:10 these verses 1 and 2 of this Psalm 24 also lays the foundation for the understanding of our relationship with God; the creator of the natural universe to whom we owe everything (*Genesis 1:1; Nehemiah 9:6; Psalm 102:25; Acts 14:5; 17:24*)

Verse 3 made it clear to man that to have entry into the kingdom of God, there is a set standard by God Himself to be met.

The standards expected of God's creatures are correspondingly high because of His holiness; hence the questions in verse 3- *'who shall ascend unto the hill of the LORD? Who shall stand in His Holy place?* (Sacred place).

God demands man's absolute purity as criteria for access into His sacred place. That is, His Kingdom. Are you pure to enter into God's Kingdom?

Requirement for God's Kingdom

The requirements needed to be able to gain access into God's Kingdom as stated in verse 4 include:

    i.   Clean hands

ii. Pure hearts and
iii. Possession of soul that hath not been lifted-up to vanity nor sworn deceitfully.

David emphasizes that those who want to worship, serve God and receive His blessings must be pursuing a pure heart and a righteous life.

"Clean hands" can therefore be said to be hands free from external acts of sin (*Isaiah 1:15; 33:15 & 1Timothy 2:8*).

A "Pure Heart" refers to inward holiness, right motives and goals. Only the pure in heart will see God (*Matthew 5:8; Isaiah 33:15-17*).

The set standards expected of God are inescapable because they form the preconditions to approaching His presence.

We must note that the purity required is both inward and outward towards God and fellowman.

However, there is a promise in verse 5 which states that those who meet the set standard required ('Clean hands', pure heart', and 'soul void of deceit') shall receive the blessing from the LORD. (*Isaiah 33:15-17*).

Verses 7 to 10 of Psalm 24 are Messianic. The 'King of Glory' referred to herein is the Lord Jesus (*John 1:14*). The 'generation' of those who seek Him (faithful believers) must pray that the 'King of Glory' should come

This prayer for God's Kingdom to come' anticipates Christ eternal reign and the final destruction of evil. (Zechariah 9:9).

Without holiness, no man shall see the LORD.

PRAYER: Lord, help me to keep my soul from what is false and deceitful in Jesus Mighty name. Amen

CHAPTER TWENTY - FIVE

I TRUST IN THEE O LORD! SHOW ME THY WAYS

BIBLE READING: **PSALM 25 (King James Version)**

Unto thee, O LORD, do I lift up my soul.

² O my God, I trust in thee: let me not be ashamed, let not mine enemies triumph over me.

³ Yea, let none that wait on thee be ashamed: let them be ashamed which transgress without cause.

⁴ Shew me thy ways, O LORD; teach me thy paths.

⁵ Lead me in thy truth, and teach me: for thou art the God of my salvation; on thee do I wait all the day.

⁶ Remember, O LORD, thy tender mercies and thy lovingkindnesses; for they have been ever of old.

⁷ Remember not the sins of my youth, nor my transgressions: according to thy mercy remember thou me for thy goodness' sake, O LORD.

⁸ Good and upright is the LORD: therefore will he teach sinners in the way.

⁹ The meek will he guide in judgment: and the meek will he teach his way.

¹⁰ *All the paths of the* LORD *are mercy and truth unto such as keep his covenant and his testimonies.*

¹¹ *For thy name's sake, O* LORD, *pardon mine iniquity; for it is great.*

¹² *What man is he that feareth the* LORD? *him shall he teach in the way that he shall choose.*

¹³ *His soul shall dwell at ease; and his seed shall inherit the earth.*

¹⁴ *The secret of the* LORD *is with them that fear him; and he will shew them his covenant.*

¹⁵ *Mine eyes are ever toward the* LORD; *for he shall pluck my feet out of the net.*

¹⁶ *Turn thee unto me, and have mercy upon me; for I am desolate and afflicted.*

¹⁷ *The troubles of my heart are enlarged: O bring thou me out of my distresses.*

¹⁸ *Look upon mine affliction and my pain; and forgive all my sins.*

¹⁹ *Consider mine enemies; for they are many; and they hate me with cruel hatred.*

²⁰ *O keep my soul, and deliver me: let me not be ashamed; for I put my trust in thee.*

²¹ *Let integrity and uprightness preserve me; for I wait on thee.*

²² Redeem Israel, O God, out of all his troubles.

PURPOSE: -   Prayer for Guidance and Protection

The Psalmist, just like Moses in Exodus 33:13 longed intensely to know God's ways. It is possible for believers to know something about God's acts (such as salvation, various miracles and so on (*Psalm 103:7*) but may never really know God either personally or intimately or understand His ways such as the role of testing, hardship, waiting on the Lord, humility, brokenness, prayer and fasting, faith, wisdom, guidance, perseverance, purity issues and the likes in relation to spiritual authority and maturity.

The basic principles for knowing God's ways in this psalm are the following:

1. We must have a sincere desire to be led into the righteous ways of God and the truth of His word (*verse 4*).
2. We must be eager to wait upon God all the time (*verse 5*).

3. We must humbly submit to God (*verse 9*) committing ourselves to godly living (*verse 10*) and fear the Lord (*verses 12 to 14*).
4. Since sin is a barrier to knowing God and His ways, we must forsake sin be cleansed and be forgiven (*verses 4 to 8*). *"If I regard iniquity in my heart, the Lord will not hear me"* (*Psalm 16:18, John 2:1-6*).
5. Adversity in our lives is not necessarily a sign of God's disfavor (*Psalm 34:19*). Knowing God and His ways may lead us into suffering and loss that we would not have otherwise encountered (See Examples of this in *Acts 14:22; 20:22-23*).

The ultimate and most perfect example of this fact is Jesus Himself, who followed God's will perfectly, yet He suffered sorrow, betrayal and persecution on the cross.

The believer, abiding in God's will must experience and expect the same suffering and loss too.

Note that in verses 1 to 7 of this psalm, David, the Psalmist used the pronouns 'I', 'My' and 'Me' about fourteen (14) times. This shows that His (Psalmist) relationship with God is very personal and very intimate.

Is your relationship with God so personal?

In verse 6 to10, the Psalmist pointed out some aspects of God's nature for two reasons:
i. To remind himself of who God is
ii. To praise and worship God – He says.

God has tender mercies; loving kindness that has been as old as God Himself.

God is upright and good (verse 8). God teaches sinners in the right path (way) God guides the week in judgments

God teaches the weak in His ways

To those who keep His covenant and testimonies, all the paths of God are truth and mercy. We need to remind ourselves constantly of who God is in order to strengthen our faith and in our firm trust in the Almighty, the all-knowing God, who is able to do everything for His children.

The good and upright Lord deals with some people in particular ways depending on their relationship with HIM (God).

From verse 11 onwards, the Psalmist is troubled by a sense of guilt among other challenges facing him; he therefore sought his help from God. In time of distress, from where or whom do you seek relief? Because he had learnt some secrets about God and His laws (verses 12 to 15).

Note the Psalmist's remorseful attitude and request from God in verse 11 to end: *'for thy name's sake, O! LORD, pardon my iniquity; for it is great"*.

In David's times of troubles or challenges and distress, he found the fault in himself, his sin and rebellion against God and His laws. Do you tend to blame others or the system when things go wrong?

Remember that God in His wisdom guides the faithful believers even in this generation of ours. Examples of such include Pastor Enoch Adejare Adeboye and Prophet Gabriel Olubunmi Fakeye among very many others.

God has a plan for every believer but His plans may be missed by any believer who ignores God's word or misinterprets it as well as him who makes decisions contrary to His will.

If the basic convictions, attitudes and teachings found in the Bible are not deeply practiced or embedded in our lives, we will miss God's destiny for us and even possibly go astray. Righteousness lies at the root of God's guidance. (*Verse 21; "Let integrity and uprightness preserve me; for I wait on thee'; Romans 8:11-14; 23:3*).

PRAYER: Show me your ways, O! LORD and teach me your paths. For thy name sake Pardon my iniquity; for it is great.

CHAPTER TWENTY - SIX
THE BASIS OF JUDGEMENT: EXAMINE ME O LORD!

BIBLE READING: **PSALM 26 (King James Version)**

Judge me, O LORD; for I have walked in mine integrity: I have trusted also in the LORD; therefore I shall not slide.

² Examine me, O LORD, and prove me; try my reins and my heart.

³ For thy lovingkindness is before mine eyes: and I have walked in thy truth.

⁴ I have not sat with vain persons, neither will I go in with dissemblers.

⁵ I have hated the congregation of evil doers; and will not sit with the wicked.

⁶ I will wash mine hands in innocency: so will I compass thine altar, O LORD:

⁷ That I may publish with the voice of thanksgiving, and tell of all thy wondrous works.

⁸ LORD, I have loved the habitation of thy house, and the place where thine honour dwelleth.

⁹ Gather not my soul with sinners, nor my life with bloody men:

¹⁰ In whose hands is mischief, and their right hand is full of bribes.

¹¹ But as for me, I will walk in mine integrity: redeem me, and be merciful unto me.

¹² My foot standeth in an even place: in the congregations will I bless the LORD.

PURPOSE: - A Prostration of Integrity can be used to intensify ones prayers to God

This Psalm, like 1st Corinthians, is a powerful challenge to the way many of us live as Christians. Pleasing God is the Psalmist's goal. His happiness does not emanate from associating with the world (*verses .4-5, 9-10*) but from being in the "house" and "congregation" of the Lord (verse 12) where God's presence and power are manifested among his people, where God's glory dwells (*Ephesians 3:21*) and where believers walk in God's truth.

The psalmist is convinced that he would win the smile of God's approval if his desire, thoughts, words and actions are subjected to close examination.

What are some negative things the Psalmist avoids? (*verses 4 and 5; compare to Psalm 1:1*)

    i.   He had not sat with vain persons (deceitful men).

    ii.   He had not moved or gone in with dissemblers (worthless people or consortium of hypocrites).

    iii.   He hated the congregation of evildoers.

    iv.   He does not sit with the wicked.

    v.   Positive habits the Psalmist cultivates a (*verses. 5 to 8, 12; compare with Psalm 1:2*).

    vi.   Washes His hands in innocence and March in worship round your altar.

vii. He sang hymns of thanksgiving.

viii. He gives testimonies of all God's wonderful deeds to people.

ix. He loves the house of God where His glory dwells.

In spite of all the Psalmist outstanding ways of living, he did not see that he merited God's salvation (*verses 9, 11; compare to Isaiah 64:6*).

This good man worships and serves God in the beauty of His holiness, because of who He is rather than for what we shall gain. We cannot bribe God, not even with our worship.

We can see the Psalmist express his strong confidence in verse 12 of this psalm.

When we live to please the LORD God, and not merely ourselves, HE gives us His peace. Isaiah 26:3 confirms this *"Thou wilt keep him in perfect peace, whose mind is stayed on thee: because he trusteth in thee"*.

Emulate the psalmist by avoiding negative habits contrary to God's rules and cultivate the positive habits like the psalmist.

PRAYER: O God, help me to live a blameless life, redeem me and be merciful to me for Jesus' sake Amen.

CHAPTER TWENTY - SEVEN
SONG OF TRUST AND CONFIDENCE IN GOD

BIBLE READING: **PSALM 27** (King James Version)

The LORD is my light and my salvation; whom shall I fear? the LORD is the strength of my life; of whom shall I be afraid?

² When the wicked, even mine enemies and my foes, came upon me to eat up my flesh, they stumbled and fell.

³ Though an host should encamp against me, my heart shall not fear: though war should rise against me, in this will I be confident.

⁴ One thing have I desired of the LORD, that will I seek after; that I may dwell in the house of the LORD all the days of my life, to behold the beauty of the LORD, and to enquire in his temple.

⁵ For in the time of trouble he shall hide me in his pavilion: in the secret of his tabernacle shall he hide me; he shall set me up upon a rock.

⁶ And now shall mine head be lifted up above mine enemies round about me: therefore will I offer in his tabernacle sacrifices of joy; I will sing, yea, I will sing praises unto the LORD.

⁷ Hear, O LORD, when I cry with my voice: have mercy also upon me, and answer me.

⁸ When thou saidst, Seek ye my face; my heart said unto thee, Thy face, LORD, will I seek.

⁹ Hide not thy face far from me; put not thy servant away in anger: thou hast been my help; leave me not, neither forsake me, O God of my salvation.

¹⁰ When my father and my mother forsake me, then the LORD will take me up.

¹¹ Teach me thy way, O LORD, and lead me in a plain path, because of mine enemies.

¹² Deliver me not over unto the will of mine enemies: for false witnesses are risen up against me, and such as breathe out cruelty.

¹³ I had fainted, unless I had believed to see the goodness of the LORD in the land of the living.

¹⁴ Wait on the LORD: be of good courage, and he shall strengthen thine heart: wait, I say, on the LORD.

PURPOSE: - For Mercy and Forgiveness, Deliverance and Redemption

We learn from the scriptures that the 'Peace' God gives us does not necessarily mean that difficulties will be absent from our lives as believers (*John 16:33*) but it assures us of overcoming all forms of difficulties, trials and tribulations. *"These things have I spoken unto you, that in me ye might have peace. In the world, ye shall have tribulations but be of good (courage) cheer; I have overcome the world".* (*John 16:33*).

Here in Psalm 27, we learn that faithfulness to God does not mean we will not have anxious moments, false accusers, or even those who literally want to destroy us. There is however, one fact established – that detractors, enemies, and evil men cannot molest 'a heart' that trusts God. (*Verses 3,14)*. Such a heart is constantly nourished through a living contact with God and is yielded to please God always (*Verses 4, 8, 11; Also see Isaiah 26:3 and Psalm 23*).

As in Psalm 26, the Psalmist seeks the presence of God confidently. It is the most important thing he values or treasures in his life and he prays for it with all his strength and singleness of purpose.

David the psalmist describes the Lord in three ways at the beginning of this psalm:

Verse 1- As his light, salvation and strength. This description of God by the psalmist actually confirms and reveals to us his confidences. (*see verses 5, 9, 10, 13 and 14*)

V.5…….'*He shall hide me in his pavilion, in the secret of His terbanacle…… HE shall set me up upon a rock".*

V.9 ….."*Thou hast be my 'help' leave me not………O God of my salvation"* v.10……."*The Lord will not forsake me, ...The Lord will take me up*", v.13….. *"I had believed to see the goodness of the Lord in the land of the living".*

V.14 . . . *"wait on the Lord, be of good courage, and he shall strengthen thine heart: wait, I say, on the Lord"* (advice by the psalmist).

All the above statements and utterances of the Psalmist are reasons for his quiet or definite assurances in God. God Himself calls us for the same purpose of seeking His face (verse 8). The Psalmist and other ministers, servants or prophets of God also advice us to seek God (see *Moses – Deuteronomy 4:29; Isaiah – Isaiah 55:6;*

Hosea – Hosea 10:12; Jesus – Luke 11:10; Paul - Acts 17).

Those who strive always to dwell in God's Holy presence are given firm assurances that no matter what trials, tribulations that come their way, the Lord will never forsake them (verses 9 to10); they have no reason for despair. This Psalm encourages us to trust the Lord completely and not be afraid. However, no matter how unfavorable the prevailing circumstance may look.

We are expected to apply this principle when our health seems to be failing, during major or minor trials, or when we feel betrayed by loved ones. Once our lives are right with God, we can trust Him to do His part.

We need to wait patiently onto the LORD.

PRAYER: God, teach me your ways.

CHAPTER TWENTY - EIGHT
MY ROCK AND MY STRENGTH

BIBLE READING: **PSALM 28 (King James Version)**

Unto thee will I cry, O LORD my rock; be not silent to me: lest, if thou be silent to me, I become like them that go down into the pit.

² Hear the voice of my supplications, when I cry unto thee, when I lift up my hands toward thy holy oracle.

³ Draw me not away with the wicked, and with the workers of iniquity, which speak peace to their neighbours, but mischief is in their hearts.

⁴ Give them according to their deeds, and according to the wickedness of their endeavours: give them after the work of their hands; render to them their desert.

⁵ Because they regard not the works of the LORD, nor the operation of his hands, he shall destroy them, and not build them up.

⁶ Blessed be the LORD, because he hath heard the voice of my supplications.

⁷ The LORD is my strength and my shield; my heart trusted in him, and I am helped: therefore my heart greatly rejoiceth; and with my song will I praise him.

⁸ The LORD is their strength, and he is the saving strength of his anointed.

⁹ Save thy people, and bless thine inheritance: feed them also, and lift them up for ever.

PURPOSE: - A Prayer for Help and Praise for Its Answer

Have you ever prayed and yet felt that God does not care?

How did you feel during the period of silence?

However if this persist, that is, if you feel that God is silent about your request in prayer, then there is need to do some check-up on your relationship with God.

God does answer prayers responding with these answer 'Yes' meaning take, "No" and "Wait" but he is not always silent.

A faithful believer may at times feel that God is not listening to his or her prayers (*verses 1 to 3*); this experience, however will not be the norm as long as we continue to draw near to God through Christ (*See Hebrews 4:16; 7:25*).

After a period of trial, the Lord will respond and help you as a shepherd cares for His sheep (*Isaiah 40:11*).

This takes us to examine and answer this question: What kind of prayer does God answer?

Remember, Jesus taught us to pray in His name to receive answers from the father (*John 14:13-14*).

Praying in Jesus' name also means praying according to His will. So we need to master and act according to Christ and God's will with absolute trust(see verse 6 and 7) signifying and stressing David's trust and confidence in God.

Also in verse 8, you can see the confirmation of the strength of the "anointed". Definitely the prayer David offered in verse 9 will be answered by God. Here, David is also teaching and reminding us that it is very necessary for us to pray for our Ministers, Pastors, Teachers, Leaders, Evangelists, Deacons and all categories of workers in God's vineyard (the church).

Looking through this Psalm, there is a prayer of help and a prayer for the wicked (compare verses 4 and 5 with verse 9).

Which of these prayers will you offer for those who hate you?

Let us remember that God is not only our refuge, strength, shield and that of vengeance but HE is our savior in whom all men and women irrespective of race or colour should trust for their salvation.

You need to call upon God, take all your problems, trials, tribulation and all sorts to God in prayer spare and spend some time with your creator. Then wait patiently on Him and see Him surprising you wonderfully.

On an ending thought, God knows when and how to fight and win life's battle for us. Let us trust HIM alone.

PRAYER: Thank you God for hearing my prayer when I call upon thee and that you have never disappointed me.

CHAPTER TWENTY - NINE
THE VOICE OF THE LORD IN THE STORM

BIBLE READING: **PSALM 29 (King James Version)**

Give unto the LORD, O ye mighty, give unto the LORD glory and strength.

² Give unto the LORD the glory due unto his name; worship the LORD in the beauty of holiness.

³ The voice of the LORD is upon the waters: the God of glory thundereth: the LORD is upon many waters.

⁴ The voice of the LORD is powerful; the voice of the LORD is full of majesty.

⁵ The voice of the LORD breaketh the cedars; yea, the LORD breaketh the cedars of Lebanon.

⁶ He maketh them also to skip like a calf; Lebanon and Sirion like a young unicorn.

⁷ The voice of the LORD divideth the flames of fire.

⁸ The voice of the LORD shaketh the wilderness; the LORD shaketh the wilderness of Kadesh.

⁹ The voice of the LORD maketh the hinds to calve, and discovereth the forests: and in his temple doth every one speak of his glory.

¹⁰ The LORD sitteth upon the flood; yea, the LORD sitteth King for ever.

¹¹ The LORD will give strength unto his people; the LORD will bless his people with peace.

PURPOSE: Ascribing Glory and Strength to the Omnipotent Lord

This Psalm is a hymn of David praising and glorifying the Omnipotent God (*verses 1 to 7*) who controls the heaven and earth; reveals Himself in nature (*verses 3 to 9*) and bless His people with strength and peace (verses 10 and 11). In this Psalm, we can see the mighty power of God in His voice on waters, in thunder storm breaking the cedars (of Lebanon), making cedars skip like a calf; God's voice dividing the flames of fire, shaking the wilderness of kadesh, making the hinds to calve and discovering the forests. The Lord sits upon floods and as King forever.

God's hand and voice can be on anything you desire Him to be involved. So God deserves and in fact is to be glorified every moment.

There is certainty that God will surely give strength to His people and bless them with peace.

It is therefore important that we give glory to God, praise and worship Him always for His mercy endures for ever on us.

In every situation, remember to glorify God always for He is in control of the whole universe, the inhabitants inclusive.

PRAYER: God, the father, give me the grace to glorify, and praise you always for you are worthy to be glorified.

CHAPTER THIRTY
THE LORD MY HELPER

BIBLE READING: **PSALM 30 (King James Version)**

I will extol thee, O LORD; for thou hast lifted me up, and hast not made my foes to rejoice over me.

² O LORD my God, I cried unto thee, and thou hast healed me.

³ O LORD, thou hast brought up my soul from the grave: thou hast kept me alive, that I should not go down to the pit.

⁴ Sing unto the LORD, O ye saints of his, and give thanks at the remembrance of his holiness.

⁵ For his anger endureth but a moment; in his favour is life: weeping may endure for a night, but joy cometh in the morning.

⁶ And in my prosperity I said, I shall never be moved.

⁷ LORD, by thy favour thou hast made my mountain to stand strong: thou didst hide thy face, and I was troubled.

⁸ I cried to thee, O LORD; and unto the LORD I made supplication.

⁹ What profit is there in my blood, when I go down to the pit? Shall the dust praise thee? shall it declare thy truth?

¹⁰ Hear, O LORD, and have mercy upon me: LORD, be thou my helper.

¹¹ Thou hast turned for me my mourning into dancing: thou hast put off my sackcloth, and girded me with gladness;

¹² To the end that my glory may sing praise to thee, and not be silent. O LORD my God, I will give thanks unto thee for ever.

PURPOSE: - For House Dedication and Thanksgiving / Praise from Deliverance from the Hands of Death

This Psalm and song is sung at the dedication of the house of David.

This Psalm is a song sang in praise of God by David. He testified to confess God's great help for him over his enemies.

He rejoiced that his enemies were put to shame and disappointed by God (verses 1 to 3) with particular reference to verse 3 which says *"O Lord, thou hast brought up my soul from the grave; thou hast kept me alive that I should not go down to the pit"*. In verse 4, David calls unto the saints (God's people) to sing praise and thank God genuinely in all situations all the time and under all circumstances.

We should for example, be able to praise God:

i. When HE is angry with us

ii. When HE leaves us in such trying situations that we even weep.

iii. When HE hides His face and remains silent.

Apostle Paul admonishes us in I Thessalonians 5:18 to give thanks in everything; for it is the will of God in Christ Jesus concerning us all.

Psalm 30, verse 6 says *"And in my prosperity....... I shall never be moved"*. Secure in his prosperity, the

Psalmist assumed that nothing could destroy his happiness.

For this reason of self –worth by the Psalmist, God then withdrew His protective hand and brought serious trouble and helplessness into his (David) life, causing him to experience the need for God's continual care and presence (verses 8 to 10).

All believers who feel secure in themselves, who rely on temporal things and who give God and His kingdom anything but first place in their lives are warned by the words of this Psalm to beware.

Remember Psalm 30 reminds and dwells us how mighty and powerful God is.

Another fact to remember is that the Lord is with us in all circumstances because He promised never to leave us alone nor forsake us.

Absolute/total dependence o God almighty can make man succeed in life.

PRAYER: Heavenly father, teach me to be thankful always in every situation either favorable or not. God teach me not to rely on my wisdom or wealth but to depend on you for all I need in all areas of my life in Jesus name. Amen.

CHAPTER THIRTY - ONE
TRUSTING OUR TIMES INTO GOD'S HANDS

BIBLE READING: PSALM 31 (King James Version)

In thee, O LORD, do I put my trust; let me never be ashamed: deliver me in thy righteousness.

² Bow down thine ear to me; deliver me speedily: be thou my strong rock, for an house of defence to save me.

³ For thou art my rock and my fortress; therefore for thy name's sake lead me, and guide me.

⁴ Pull me out of the net that they have laid privily for me: for thou art my strength.

⁵ Into thine hand I commit my spirit: thou hast redeemed me, O LORD God of truth.

⁶ I have hated them that regard lying vanities: but I trust in the LORD.

⁷ I will be glad and rejoice in thy mercy: for thou hast considered my trouble; thou hast known my soul in adversities;

⁸ And hast not shut me up into the hand of the enemy: thou hast set my feet in a large room.

⁹ *Have mercy upon me, O LORD, for I am in trouble: mine eye is consumed with grief, yea, my soul and my belly.*

¹⁰ *For my life is spent with grief, and my years with sighing: my strength faileth because of mine iniquity, and my bones are consumed.*

¹¹ *I was a reproach among all mine enemies, but especially among my neighbours, and a fear to mine acquaintance: they that did see me without fled from me.*

¹² *I am forgotten as a dead man out of mind: I am like a broken vessel.*

¹³ *For I have heard the slander of many: fear was on every side: while they took counsel together against me, they devised to take away my life.*

¹⁴ *But I trusted in thee, O LORD: I said, Thou art my God.*

¹⁵ *My times are in thy hand: deliver me from the hand of mine enemies, and from them that persecute me.*

¹⁶ *Make thy face to shine upon thy servant: save me for thy mercies' sake.*

¹⁷ *Let me not be ashamed, O LORD; for I have called upon thee: let the wicked be ashamed, and let them be silent in the grave.*

¹⁸ *Let the lying lips be put to silence; which speak grievous things proudly and contemptuously against the righteous.*

[19] *Oh how great is thy goodness, which thou hast laid up for them that fear thee; which thou hast wrought for them that trust in thee before the sons of men!*

[20] *Thou shalt hide them in the secret of thy presence from the pride of man: thou shalt keep them secretly in a pavilion from the strife of tongues.*

[21] *Blessed be the LORD: for he hath shewed me his marvellous kindness in a strong city.*

[22] *For I said in my haste, I am cut off from before thine eyes: nevertheless thou heardest the voice of my supplications when I cried unto thee.*

[23] *O love the LORD, all ye his saints: for the LORD preserveth the faithful, and plentifully rewardeth the proud doer.*

[24] *Be of good courage, and he shall strengthen your heart, all ye that hope in the LORD.*

PURPOSE: - A cry for help when in distress and an assurance that God will respond to my cries.

Distress is a common thing to the modern man. Apostle Paul foretold the times we are in as the 'times of distresses.

A period of distress is a very difficult time as denoted by the Greek word "kalepos" meaning difficult times.

These difficult periods are times when vices abound and virtues are wanting. They are periods when we sometimes feel that evil powers and influences dominate our lives. They come in form of unfaithful friends, vicious enemies; corrupt leaders and politicians, vindictive rulers or bosses, inefficient and incompetent workers and obviously insincere fellow believers.

This situation was also common in the times of old as it is now. These experiences often tend to determine the way we live, dictate what and how we believe, act and generally keep us in fear.

The psalmist (David) here in Psalm 31 began by pleading that God should and will certainly take away his shame (*verse 3*). He emphasized that God alone is his rock and fortress. Ephesians 6:11 warns us that we are in a spiritual warfare that rages all the time. We therefore must be fully aware of these enemies and be equally determined to face those enemies in prayers.

However, we should note that this is not a call to see everybody as enemies and every situation as the manifestation of evil forces. It is a call to spiritual alertness that recognizes the strategies of the devil; learn to avoid being taken unawares. It is asking us to be discerning so that we don't shoot at the wrong or non-existent targets.

David, the author of this psalm, gives us a good example of how to handle the times of distress, difficulty and tribulations.
What did he do?
The first step he took was to pray to God, expressing deeply how he felt with his compounded problems (*verses 1 to 5; 9 to 13*). Prophet Jeremiah used this phrase from verse 13 to express his sorrow and stress (*Jeremiah 6:25 and 20:10*). You can read verse 5 of this Psalm 31 again and connect it with the last prayer of Jesus Christ our Lord on the cross which says, *"Father, into thy hands I commit my spirit"* (*Luke 23:46*). These words have often been used by faithful believers in their dying hours (*Acts 7: 5-9*).These

words express total dependency on God and faith in His goodness to His people. (*Romans 8:28*).

Furtherance to the first step, David steered clear from the wicked although evil was popular. Christians and believers should steer clear of the wicked, all wicked acts and most importantly be watchful to live Holy lives (*verses 6 to 8*). We need the special grace of God to cope and we have to ask for it (*verse 9*) coupled with total trust in the Lord (*verse 14*) and total submission to His will (*verse 5 and 15*).

To commit ourselves into God's care is equally necessary during times of danger, trials, tribulations and distress. This we can see was the first thing David did. We need God's guidance and direction to resolve the problems of our shame otherwise we ended up drowning ourselves in self-pity and unworthiness.

However, we must learn to be grateful to God in praises, worship, thanksgiving and prayers for the good things He (GOD) has done for us and in storing up for us (verse 19). We may indeed go through difficult times but they will deepen our love and understanding of God who preserved the faithful (verse 23). We should therefore be ready to encourage other people passing through difficult or hard times (*verses 23 and 24*). We are bound to overcome if we follow these two principles of David.

It is however noteworthy to take these two steps:
i. Depart from those who cling to idols and those who practice or carry out acts of wickedness such as blackmailing, assassination, mockery and the likes.
ii. Commit yourself and ways totally into the hands of God the creator and the all knowing.

PRAYER: My God, I thank you that in you and with you we are always safe and that when we are in anguish or distress of shame, you restore and relieve us.
Thank you LORD for setting me free from the trap that is set for me in all areas of my life.

CHAPTER THIRTY - TWO
THE JOYS OF BEING FORGIVEN

BIBLE READING: PSALM 32 (King James Version)

Blessed is he whose transgression is forgiven, whose sin is covered.

² Blessed is the man unto whom the LORD imputeth not iniquity, and in whose spirit there is no guile.

³ When I kept silence, my bones waxed old through my roaring all the day long.

⁴ For day and night thy hand was heavy upon me: my moisture is turned into the drought of summer. Selah.

⁵ I acknowledge my sin unto thee, and mine iniquity have I not hid. I said, I will confess my transgressions unto the LORD; and thou forgavest the iniquity of my sin. Selah.

⁶ For this shall every one that is godly pray unto thee in a time when thou mayest be found: surely in the floods of great waters they shall not come nigh unto him.

⁷ Thou art my hiding place; thou shalt preserve me from trouble; thou shalt compass me about with songs of deliverance. Selah.

⁸ I will instruct thee and teach thee in the way which thou shalt go: I will guide thee with mine eye.

⁹ Be ye not as the horse, or as the mule, which have no understanding: whose mouth must be held in with bit and bridle, lest they come near unto thee.

¹⁰ Many sorrows shall be to the wicked: but he that trusteth in the LORD, mercy shall compass him about.

¹¹ Be glad in the LORD, and rejoice, ye righteous: and shout for joy, all ye that are upright in heart.

PURPOSE: - A Prayer in Time of Distress/Stress

This is an exciting journey from darkness (sin) to light (pardon), and a recipe for confidence and growth in the Lord.

David the Psalmist teaches us more lessons to learn about 'times of stress and distress. Verse one of this Psalms says and I quote, *"Blessed is he whose transgression (sins) is forgiven*! The only truly happy people are those who have received forgiveness of their sins from God so that the guilt of their transgressions (sins) that weighs upon their minds and consciences are erased totally and makes them enjoy the peace of God.

Such blessed peace is open to all sinners who come to the Lord (*Matthew 11: 28-29*).

The Psalmist describes God's forgiveness in three ways:
i. He (God) forgives sins (Pardons it).
ii. He (God) covers the sins (Puts it out of sight).
iii. The sin(s) is not imputed (the guilt of the sin is cancelled from record).

"... *imputeth not iniquity*. . . " (verse 2). To explain this verse, Paul the apostle in the book of Romans Chapter 4 and verses 6 to 8 quotes verse 1 to 2 of this Psalm to show that God treats sincerely, repentant sinners as righteous, not because righteousness is something that you earn through work, but rather is received as a gift when confession of sins are made and one believes in the Lord (*verse 5*).

In this Psalm, David teaches us that when in distress, trials or tribulations, it is good to search our lives and be sure it is free of any offence towards God or man. Often times we look handsome, beautiful, and radiant outside (physically appearance) but inside we are wasting away because of sin. With a life that clings to sin, there can be no peace or joy in Him. The Psalmist here in this Psalter experienced the joy of forgiven sins and covered transgressions (*verse 1*). This is an exciting journey from darkness (sin) to light (pardon) and a recipe for confidence of growth in the Lord. Again, this is what keeps one going in a time of stress.

Guilt (of sin) can cause all sorts of sickness and disease in the body (verses 2 to 5); this is the agony and penalty that concealed sin brings. What we need in this type of situation is to acknowledge, confess with an honest, sincere, repentant heart and forsake our sins before God (verse 5).

Such actions immediately open the gate of special blessings, described by David in verse one of this Psalm. That is, the forgiven sinner will receive God's gracious pardon, the removal of guilt and the gift of His abiding presence.

This is the beginning of a whole new life of guidance (*verse 6*), protection (*verse 7*), and instruction (*verse 8*) from the Lord.

God is interested in giving you a new beginning; let His word instruct and teach you what to do.

These words are not rules and regulations to restrict and limit you. They are God's words that will give you the sense of the grace and unfailing love of God that will enable you to do what you think is impossible.

Praying to God where He may be found

Another important issue raised by the Psalmist here in this Psalter is praying to God where He may be found (*verse 6*). God is not found just in any place. There are some places that are clearly filthy for God to be found such as in brothels, shrines, beer joints to mention but a few.

We should be careful to keep company with the Godly, and serve Him in spirit and in truth (*Read Psalm 24:3 to 7*).

God desires to fellowship with us and we should seek Him early, always and earnestly (*Psalm 62:1*) while He may be found (*Isaiah 55:6*) and in the shelter of this high place. (*Psalm 91:1*).

With the PROMISES in verse 8 which says, *"I will instruct thee, and teach thee in the way which thou shall go, I will guide thee with mine eyes"*, and the warnings in verse 9 - *"Be ye not as the horse or as the mule, which have no understanding; whose mouth must be held in with bit and bridle, lest they come near unto thee"*. Both the promise and the warning must be taken together for the Lord has made this promise and given the warning to a forgiven believer who has a teachable spirit; treasures God's presence and counsel (*verse 7*) and continues to be upright in heart (*verse 11*).

In PRAISING and WORSHIPING God, you find strength and victory. So PRAISE HIM ALWAYS!

Acknowledge, confess, and forsake your SINS with honest and sincere repentant heart before God Almighty.

PRAYER: God, I know that my sorrow will be taken, so give me the grace to PRAISE and WORSHIP you all the days of my life, and in every circumstance that I may find myself in Jesus name. Amen.

CHAPTER THIRTY - THREE
QUALIFIED BY GRACE

BIBLE READING: **PSALM 33 (King James Version)**

Rejoice in the LORD, O ye righteous: for praise is comely for the upright.

² Praise the LORD with harp: sing unto him with the psaltery and an instrument of ten strings.

³ Sing unto him a new song; play skilfully with a loud noise.

⁴ For the word of the LORD is right; and all his works are done in truth.

⁵ He loveth righteousness and judgment: the earth is full of the goodness of the LORD.

⁶ By the word of the LORD were the heavens made; and all the host of them by the breath of his mouth.

⁷ He gathereth the waters of the sea together as an heap: he layeth up the depth in storehouses.

⁸ Let all the earth fear the LORD: let all the inhabitants of the world stand in awe of him.

⁹ For he spake, and it was done; he commanded, and it stood fast.

10 The LORD *bringeth the counsel of the heathen to nought: he maketh the devices of the people of none effect.*

11 The counsel of the LORD *standeth for ever, the thoughts of his heart to all generations.*

12 Blessed is the nation whose God is the LORD*; and the people whom he hath chosen for his own inheritance.*

13 The LORD *looketh from heaven; he beholdeth all the sons of men.*

14 From the place of his habitation he looketh upon all the inhabitants of the earth.

15 He fashioneth their hearts alike; he considereth all their works.

16 There is no king saved by the multitude of an host: a mighty man is not delivered by much strength.

17 An horse is a vain thing for safety: neither shall he deliver any by his great strength.

18 Behold, the eye of the LORD *is upon them that fear him, upon them that hope in his mercy;*

19 To deliver their soul from death, and to keep them alive in famine.

20 Our soul waiteth for the LORD*: he is our help and our shield.*

21 For our heart shall rejoice in him, because we have trusted in his holy name.

²² *Let thy mercy, O LORD, be upon us, according as we hope in thee.*

PURPOSE: - A Prayer of Praise and Encouragement

In psalm 33, we are made to understand that only 'the righteous' have the guts to praise the Lord or can confidently sing praises to God.

It is good and appreciated if the man praising God can do it accompanied with some musical instruments such as guitar, tambourine, drums, trumpets and other melodious musical instruments. Verse 2 of this psalm says, *'Sing unto Him with the psaltery and an instrument of ten strings"*.

It is not only with these instruments should you praise God, it is demanded that one should be skillful in the playing of at least an instrument and must be able to sing 'a new song' always with a 'loud voice' unto the Lord (*verses 2 and 3*).

We are made qualified to do so by the Grace accomplished through the death of Jesus Christ alone.

In verses 4, 6 and 9, the Psalmist tells us that the WORD of the LORD is right. By these words the heavens were made and the entire host, by 'the breath of His mouth'.

The breath of God is thus equivalent to the activity of God's spirit. An important biblical truth is in this verse 6 ; the union of the power of God's spirit by exercise or through the operation of Faith or putting Faith into action always which releases the creative power of God on behalf of His people for God spoke and it was done, He commanded and it stood fast (Genesis 1:1-end; Genesis 2). So we need to ask in FAITH and consider it done.

In verses 5 and 11, what God loves are clearly stated for us. God does not only love our 'praises', He is delighted in our righteousness and uprightness; living an unpolluted life.

It is quite comforting to read in verses 13 and 14 that the Lord looks down from heaven and sees all mankind including you: He (God) is the all-seeing God, present everywhere and thus referred to as the 'omnipresent, omnipotent and omniscience'.

What does God see in you, your thoughts, activities, family, church, community country and nation?

Remember as in verse 16, that a mighty is not saved nor delivered by much strength. No king can save himself by his strength. While 'the eye of the Lord is upon all people (verses 1 and 14), it rests in a special way on those who 'fear Him'. Psalm 34:15 confirms this, *"The eyes of the LORD are upon the righteous and His ears are open unto their cry"* (*Psalm 10:17; Isaiah 30:19; Jeremiah 33:3*).

Why? To deliver the souls of the righteous from death (*verse 19*) and to keep them alive from famine. For instance, Joseph was taken care of before, during and after famine in Egypt. We must therefore cease or desist from engaging ourselves in any acts of crime, violence, wickedness, etc if the 'grace of God' is to work for us.

'God's eye' refer to God's caring love and providential oversight of our lives *'To deliver their soul from death, and to keep them alive in famine'* means that as long as we fear the Lord, put our hope in Him, wait for Him and remain in His will, HE will watch over and protect us. So we will not die unless it is according to His (God's) plan. It is therefore imperative to wait patiently according to verse 20 for what God will do. To wait patiently on God implies that you will exercise faith and trust in HIM.

Praise the Lord always with a thankful heart for this is good and rewarding.

Let your soul wait for the Lord, for He is our very help and shield that does not fail in all circumstances.

PRAYER POINT: O God, enlist me in your army of missionaries taking your name to places as your kingdom is advancing to all lands and nations in Jesus name. Amen.

Lord, give me the patience to be able to wait on you in faith, trust and to receive abundantly your Holy Spirit and divine direction to my daily living in Jesus name. Amen.

CHAPTER THIRTY - FOUR

THE TESTIMONY OF GOD'S GOODNESS AT ALL TIMES

BIBLE READING: PSALM 34 (King James Version)

I will bless the LORD at all times: his praise shall continually be in my mouth.

² My soul shall make her boast in the LORD: the humble shall hear thereof, and be glad.

³ O magnify the LORD with me, and let us exalt his name together.

⁴ I sought the LORD, and he heard me, and delivered me from all my fears.

⁵ They looked unto him, and were lightened: and their faces were not ashamed.

⁶ This poor man cried, and the LORD heard him, and saved him out of all his troubles.

⁷ The angel of the LORD encampeth round about them that fear him, and delivereth them.

⁸ O taste and see that the LORD is good: blessed is the man that trusteth in him.

⁹ *O fear the* LORD, *ye his saints: for there is no want to them that fear him.*

¹⁰ *The young lions do lack, and suffer hunger: but they that seek the* LORD *shall not want any good thing.*

¹¹ *Come, ye children, hearken unto me: I will teach you the fear of the* LORD.

¹² *What man is he that desireth life, and loveth many days, that he may see good?*

¹³ *Keep thy tongue from evil, and thy lips from speaking guile.*

¹⁴ *Depart from evil, and do good; seek peace, and pursue it.*

¹⁵ *The eyes of the* LORD *are upon the righteous, and his ears are open unto their cry.*

¹⁶ *The face of the* LORD *is against them that do evil, to cut off the remembrance of them from the earth.*

¹⁷ *The righteous cry, and the* LORD *heareth, and delivereth them out of all their troubles.*

¹⁸ *The* LORD *is nigh unto them that are of a broken heart; and saveth such as be of a contrite spirit.*

¹⁹ *Many are the afflictions of the righteous: but the* LORD *delivereth him out of them all.*

²⁰ *He keepeth all his bones: not one of them is broken.*

²¹ *Evil shall slay the wicked: and they that hate the righteous shall be desolate.*

*²² The L*ORD *redeemeth the soul of his servants: and none of them that trust in him shall be desolate.*

PURPOSE: - To Praise and trust in God to deliver one from troubles

This Psalter is a song sung by David when he changed his behavior before Abimelech who drove him away and he departed.

"I will bless the LORD at 'all' times; His praise shall continually be in my mouth" (*verse 1*). From the quoted verse, the writers determined to praise and exalt God at 'all times' for a miraculous deliverance from great trouble. This is a good example for us to follow. Why? This is because his testimonies encourage all afflicted believers to believe that they may also experience the goodness of God.

The Psalmist testified also to the fact that when 'he sought the Lord, He (God) delivered him from all his fears (*verse 4)* just as the poor man was saved out of all his troubles (*verses 6,17and 19*).

David the Psalmist in verse 7 also testified that the promise of divine intervention by God, reserved only for those who truly fear God was made available to Him when he said that the angel of the Lord encamp roundabout they that fear him and He delivers them.

This mean that the angelic host of heaven which are ministering spirits are sent to protect them and those who fear the Lord that are in similar situations. These are heirs to salvation (Hebrew 1:14; II Kings 6:16-17; Genesis 32:1-2).

Are you one of the heirs of salvation?

Do you fear and believe God?

There are promises in the Psalm and they are conditional and reserved only for those who genuinely fear the LORD.

The promises includes but are not limited to the following; to deliver us from fear (*verse 4*), to save us from troubles (*verses 6 and 17*), to send angels to encamp around us (*verse 7*), to supply our needs (*verse 9*), to give us abundant life (*verse 12*), to hear our prayers (*verse 15*), to comfort us with His presence (*verse 18*) and to redeem our soul (*verse 22*).

These promises will be ours if we candidly seek the Lord (*verses 4 and 10*), cry out to Him (*verse 6*), draw close to Him and fear Him (*verses 7 and 9*).

We are also to keep our tongues from the evil of lying (*verse 13*); remain separated from the evil world (*verse 14*); have contrite a heart (*verse 18*) and become His servant (*verse 22*).

It is thereafter that the praise in verse 9 - *"there is no want to them that fear him"* - will manifest in our life.

It is worthy of note that the psalmist – David, determined to exalt the LORD God at "all times". This is a very good example to emulate.

Some Testimonies:

David testified to the following:

    a. When he (David) sought the Lord, the Lord delivered him from all his troubles and fears (*verse 4*).

    b. Just as the poor man was saved of all his troubles, David too was saved by God (*verse 6*).

c. The Lord gives good things at all times (*verse 10*).
   d. The Lord grants many good days to all those who hate evil and do good (*verses 12, 14 and 16*).
   e. God protects all our bones. Here we can see God's perfect protection against all bone breaking accidents (*verse 20*).

Can you also give the above testimonies of all good things the Lord has done for you?

Have you tasted the Lord's goodness in your past years?

Do you pray or wish to experience the Lord's goodness and mercies in your life?

Why not seek the Lord like the Psalmist, David (*verse 4*) and allow only God to fulfill his promise of verse 11; remember He has promised to teach you His fears. Always be conscious of these things:

i. That He will give many good days to all those who hate and do not partake in evil but do good (*verse 18*).
ii. He shall redeem the soul of His servants and all that trust Him shall never be desolate (*verse 21*).
iii. Evil shall slay the wicked; and they that hate the righteous shall be desolate (*verse 21*).

It is worthy to note or pay particular attention to verse 19 of this Psalm 34 which says *"Many are the afflictions of the righteous; but the Lord delivereth him out of them all"*. This is an assurance to the believers and verse 5 of this Psalm is grace and blessing of God to them.

In the Bible, God promised blessings and prosperity for those who obey His law (*Deuteronomy 28:1 to 14*), yet alongside these promises are the realities (*verse 15 to the end*) of the consequences of disobeying God's law. It should be noted that in actual fact *'many are the afflictions of the righteous'* (*Hebrews 11:33-38*). Therefore, believing in God and living a righteous life will not keep us from troubles and sufferings in this world. On the contrary, commitment to God often brings tests and persecutions (*Matthew 5:10*).

- ❖ God has ordained that we must go through many hardships to enter His Kingdom (*Acts 14:22; I Corinthians 15:19; II Timothy 3:12*).
- ❖ The suffering of 'the righteous' must be counter balanced by the revelation that the Lord wishes to deliver us out of all our afflictions. When the purpose in permitting affliction is accomplished, He (God) then delivers us from them (the wicked) either by direct or supernatural intervention in this world and life (*Hebrews 11:33-35*), or big victorious death and transference to the life hereafter (Hebrews 11:35-37).

Let us therefore strive to live in accordance to God's law despite all tempting situations and hold fast unto God the Almighty who cannot fail us.

PRAYER: God, I thank you for your care for me (us) more than I can understand.

Dear God, in my testing and persecutions give me the grace and strength to hold on to my commitment to you and deliver me from all afflictions in Jesus name I pray. Amen

CHAPTER THIRTYY - FIVE
A PRAYER OF RESCUE FROM ENEMIES

BIBLE READING: **PSALM 35 (King James Version)**

Plead my cause, O LORD, with them that strive with me: fight against them that fight against me.

² Take hold of shield and buckler, and stand up for mine help.

³ Draw out also the spear, and stop the way against them that persecute me: say unto my soul, I am thy salvation.

⁴ Let them be confounded and put to shame that seek after my soul: let them be turned back and brought to confusion that devise my hurt.

⁵ Let them be as chaff before the wind: and let the angel of the LORD chase them.

⁶ Let their way be dark and slippery: and let the angel of the LORD persecute them.

⁷ For without cause have they hid for me their net in a pit, which without cause they have digged for my soul.

⁸ Let destruction come upon him at unawares; and let his net that he hath hid catch himself: into that very destruction let him fall.

⁹ And my soul shall be joyful in the LORD*: it shall rejoice in his salvation.*

¹⁰ All my bones shall say, LORD*, who is like unto thee, which deliverest the poor from him that is too strong for him, yea, the poor and the needy from him that spoileth him?*

¹¹ False witnesses did rise up; they laid to my charge things that I knew not.

¹² They rewarded me evil for good to the spoiling of my soul.

¹³ But as for me, when they were sick, my clothing was sackcloth: I humbled my soul with fasting; and my prayer returned into mine own bosom.

¹⁴ I behaved myself as though he had been my friend or brother: I bowed down heavily, as one that mourneth for his mother.

¹⁵ But in mine adversity they rejoiced, and gathered themselves together: yea, the abjects gathered themselves together against me, and I knew it not; they did tear me, and ceased not:

¹⁶ With hypocritical mockers in feasts, they gnashed upon me with their teeth.

¹⁷ Lord, how long wilt thou look on? rescue my soul from their destructions, my darling from the lions.

¹⁸ I will give thee thanks in the great congregation: I will praise thee among much people.

¹⁹ Let not them that are mine enemies wrongfully rejoice over me: neither let them wink with the eye that hate me without a cause.

²⁰ For they speak not peace: but they devise deceitful matters against them that are quiet in the land.

²¹ Yea, they opened their mouth wide against me, and said, Aha, aha, our eye hath seen it.

²² This thou hast seen, O LORD: keep not silence: O Lord, be not far from me.

²³ Stir up thyself, and awake to my judgment, even unto my cause, my God and my Lord.

²⁴ Judge me, O LORD my God, according to thy righteousness; and let them not rejoice over me.

²⁵ Let them not say in their hearts, Ah, so would we have it: let them not say, We have swallowed him up.

²⁶ Let them be ashamed and brought to confusion together that rejoice at mine hurt: let them be clothed with shame and dishonour that magnify themselves against me.

²⁷ Let them shout for joy, and be glad, that favour my righteous cause: yea, let them say continually, Let the LORD be magnified, which hath pleasure in the prosperity of his servant.

²⁸ And my tongue shall speak of thy righteousness and of thy praise all the day long.

PURPOSE: i. Prayer for deliverance from injustice, crime and oppression.

    ii. An appeal to God to administer justice and send penalties upon the wicked that are commensurate with their crime.

Psalm thirty-five is called an 'imprecatory' psalm. What this means is that the Psalmist prays that God should bring judgment upon the enemies of His people and overthrow the wicked. (*See Psalms 35; 69; 109; 137; Nehemiah 6:14; 13:29; Jeremiah 15:15; 17:18; Galatians 5:12; II Timothy 4:14 and Revelation 6:10*).

One wonders why David prays this way. In fact this Psalter is misunderstood by many Christians, who see it as a curse from David to his enemies and contrary to teach us to pray for the salvation of our enemies and also forgive them (*Matthew 5:43-48 and Luke 23:34*).

However, a time comes in our daily lives when we must pray for evil to cease and for justice to be done for the innocent. We should be virtually concerned about the victims of cruelty, oppression and evil.

To really understand this prayer in Psalm 35, we need to know what ***imprecatory*** prayers and or psalms are. They are:

1. Prayers for deliverance from injustice, crime, and oppression. Believers have a right to pray for God's protection from evil people.
2. Appeals to God to administer justice and send penalties upon the wicked that are commensurate with their crimes (*Psalm 28:4*). If just retribution is not undertaken by God or by man's government, violence and chaos will reign in the society. (*Deuteronomy 25:1-3; Romans 13:3-4*).
3. Prayers that commit vengeance into the hands of God by the person offering them (*Deuteronomy 32:35; Proverbs 20:22; Romans 12:9*).
4. Prayers or Psalms that points to the truth that when iniquity of the wicked reaches its full measures, the

Lord in His righteousness does judge and destroys (*Genesis 15:16; Leviticus 18:24; Revelation 6:10, 17*).

5. Prayers or Psalms that inspire words of the Holy Spirit (*I Timothy 3:16-17; II Peter 1:19 - 21*) and not just an expression of the human desire of the Psalmist.

6. Prayers whose ultimate goal s seeing injustice and cruelty come to an end, evil destroyed, Satan defeated, Godliness exalted, righteousness established and the kingdom of God realized. This goal is a dominant concern in the New Testament. Jesus Christ Himself stated that true believers may pray for the vindication of the righteous. An example is the widow's prayer to 'Avenge me of my adversary' in Luke 18:3; is answered by Jesus assurance that God will avenge his own elect which cry day and night unto him". (*Luke. 18:7; Revelation 6:9-10*).

7. In imprecatory prayers, believers must keep these Biblical principles in balance;

a. The desire to see all people come to a saving knowledge of Jesus Christ (*II Peter 3:9*).
b. The desire to see evil destroyed and the kingdom of God victorious.

What then do we do?
a. We must pray earnestly for the salvation of the lost and weep for those who reject the gospel.
b. We as believers must know that goodness, righteousness and love will NEVER be established according to God's purpose until evil is conquered and Satan and his followers are forever defeated (*Revelation 19-21*).
c. The faithful must pray 'tirelessly' until the Lord Jesus Christ comes - even so come Lord Jesus (Revelation 22:20) as God's ultimate and final solution for evil in the world.

FURTHER INSIGHT INTO PSALM 35

Now having understood what an '**IMPRECATORY**' prayer or psalm is, we can see that this Psalter by the Psalmist is quite in order and should not be misunderstood in any negative perspective. Rather,

Christians and believers should see it as awareness that it is their responsibility to fight a total war on all satanic activities and devices such as oppression, injustice and all forms of wickedness.

They (believers) are to approach God Almighty with humility and all sincerity on all issues facing them.

Some important facts that we must take cognizance of in Psalm 35 are highlighted below:

i. The prayer was not offered to man but to God. The Psalmist spoke to God and expressed how it feels to be humiliated and haunted by foes (enemies) without causes. Note that David did not mention any name here. He was only praying against the activities of evil and wicked men.

   Now can you answer this question? Would you continue to pray for the success of armed robbers, witches, wizards, assassins and the likes in their operations when they spell doom for innocent citizens?

ii. The wicked here is under God's condemnation already. All through the scriptures (Bible), the poor and the needy, (verse 10), the widow, orphans and the sick always have special place in the heart of God. Anyone who maltreats any of the above mentioned is in trouble with God (*Matthew 25:31-46*).

iii. Also the Psalmist in this Psalter interceded for his persecutors when they were in trouble (*verses 12 to 14*). God did not answer his prayers on them and yet he did not give up on them; He wept for them. But what was their response or reaction to David? Verse 15 said they 'object gathered' themselves against him - paying David evil for good.

iv. God is glorified in our victory and we are blessed while Satan is put to shame (*verse 9*). We should therefore pray until our joy is full over the oppressing workers of iniquity.

v. David could claim innocence of the charges against him (*verses 1, 11 and 12*). - . . . *"Plead my cause O LORD, with them that strive with me……….."*

vi. The psalmist's relationship with the people was one of love and sacrifice (*verses 13 and 14*).

Poser – Looking through the facts in Numbers iv and vi, how much of these have characterized your own relationships?

Relationship of Psalm 35 to Man's daily Behavior (Flesh at Work)

It is worthy to note verse 17 of Psalm 35 which says, *"Lord, how long will thou look on? Rescue my soul from their destruction…"*

The words of this verse are actually true of man's reaction when he finds himself in a defenseless situation.

The wicked, oppressors and the likes pursue their malicious attack. It seems to man that God knows about it but He seems not to do anything to halt the march of their successful aggression and so the unequal struggle continues.

For us and the David, whenever we find ourselves in such position that defies logical explanation, there is need or a good reason to exercise our right of son ship by complaining to God earnestly, positioning all our questions to Him (God). Should you think this is necessary, you must never doubt God for He is always with us in all our struggles.

The struggles may be short or long termed. At times, God may allow some of our battles to overcome us because He wants to teach us certain lessons and help give us a lifting to win more important ones for His glory, our blessing and to Satan's shame or He may want us to show that we are no fair-weather Christians.

Never think that being a Christian will make all things easy. No, we have to put on the armour of God and be ready to fight a good fight of faith (*Ephesians 6:1-16*).

Therefore let us all ensure that our ultimate aim is to seek God's praise and glory (*Psalm 35:18, 27-28*).

Remember, God alone rescues the poor from those too strong for them (*verse 10; Psalm50:15*). Always pray to God and not to man (*Psalm 119:170, Proverbs 20:22*)

The battle may be long but victory is sure (*I John 5:4; I Corinthian 15:57*).

Remember, God promises to answer us when we call upon Him (*Jeremiah 33:3. Isaiah 30:19*).

Victory Verses

"For whosoever is born of God overcometh the world; and is the victory that overcometh the world, even our faith" *(I John 5:4)*

"Thanks be to God! He gives me the victory through our Lord Jesus Christ" (*I Corinthians 15:57*).

In conclusion, my brethren, be strong in the Lord and in the power of His might. "This is the VICTORY, stronger than anything, my VICTORY is FAITH and it comes from God.

PRAYERPOINTS: O God, I pray that you will grant me the strength to love you the more and love my fellow human.

Lord, please grant that I have no other ambition in all of my life's struggles than to glorify your name.

O God, give me the wisdom to pray to you in my struggles when I am in a position or situation that defies logical explanation.

CHAPTER THIRTY - SIX
THE STEADFAST LOVE OF GOD IN THE FACE OF WICKEDNESS

BIBLE READING: **PSALM 36 (King James Version)**

The transgression of the wicked saith within my heart, that there is no fear of God before his eyes.

² For he flattereth himself in his own eyes, until his iniquity be found to be hateful.

³ The words of his mouth are iniquity and deceit: he hath left off to be wise, and to do good.

⁴ He deviseth mischief upon his bed; he setteth himself in a way that is not good; he abhorreth not evil.

⁵ Thy mercy, O LORD, is in the heavens; and thy faithfulness reacheth unto the clouds.

⁶ Thy righteousness is like the great mountains; thy judgments are a great deep: O LORD, thou preservest man and beast.

⁷ How excellent is thy lovingkindness, O God! therefore the children of men put their trust under the shadow of thy wings.

⁸ They shall be abundantly satisfied with the fatness of thy house; and thou shalt make them drink of the river of thy pleasures.

⁹ For with thee is the fountain of life: in thy light shall we see light.

¹⁰ O continue thy lovingkindness unto them that know thee; and thy righteousness to the upright in heart.

¹¹ Let not the foot of pride come against me, and let not the hand of the wicked remove me.

¹² There are the workers of iniquity fallen: they are cast down, and shall not be able to rise.

PURPOSE: - Acknowledging God's unflinching love.

The word 'evil refers to basic evil and human depravity. The ungodly do not hate evil.
Hatred of sin is an essential feature of God's character (Proverbs 6:16; Jeremiah 44:4; Habakkuk 1:13). It is a fundamental aspect of Christ's ministry and kingship (*Psalm 45:7, Hebrews 1:9*).

People may be loving, kind and do good to the poor, yet if they have no indignation against wrong competent for the world's immoral ways, zeal for justice or hatred of evil, they have failed to stand with God or follow the Holy spirit (*Galatians 5:16-24*).

"*Ye that love the Lord hate evil* (Psalm 97:10) says the Bible.

This psalm of David can be seen from two dimensions:
   i.   Wickedness confronting God's love (Verses 1-4)
   ii. The steadfast love of God.

The wicked confronts God's love (verses 1-4)

This psalm confirms to us, the characteristics of the wicked and important facts about the wicked. The wicked believes that everything begins and ends with them; they see themselves as all-in-all. The wicked in their zone feel safe and secure in their nefarious activities; what a pretentions life they (wicked) lived and are still living.

It is interesting and amazing to know that heaven is aware that all the wicked does is sinful and is recorded against him them but surprisingly the wicked flatters himself, loves sin, (*verse 2*) speaks wicked, deceitful, foolish and evil words; (*verse 3*) devise mischief upon their beds and sit themselves in bad ways and rejoice at others sorrows (*verse 4*).

The wicked forgets that all that goes round comes around. The wicked who are workers of iniquity always fall down, they shall not be able to rise again as they are cast down by God (verse 12).

The Steadfast Love of God (Verses 5-11)

In contrast to the above, we read and are made to understand in verse 5-11 that the loving kindness of God is excellent. This love is linked with righteousness and truth. It is a love that seeks to preserve and enhance others rather than exploit and destroy them. It is an invitation to a continual feast of His goodness.

Examine yourself, do you think your love is also open to everybody and not just a few that can reciprocate whatever you do to them?

It is good and wise to pattern your life and your relationship with God in truth and righteousness.
Always yearn and desire to receive God's invitation to a continual feast of His goodness and enjoy His unflinching love.

PRAYER: O God, Shed your light on me daily till eternity and let me see your light to live in righteousness and truth even in the face of all odds in Jesus name. Amen.

Heavenly father, continue to show and shower your love to those who love and know you and thy righteousness to the upright in heart. Do not let them falter in Jesus name Amen.

CHAPTER THIRTY - SEVEN
THE INSECURITY OF THE WICKED AND BLESSINGS OF THE RIGHTEOUS

BIBLE READING: PSALM 37 (King James Version)

Fret not thyself because of evildoers, neither be thou envious against the workers of iniquity.

² For they shall soon be cut down like the grass, and wither as the green herb.

³ Trust in the LORD, and do good; so shalt thou dwell in the land, and verily thou shalt be fed.

⁴ Delight thyself also in the LORD: and he shall give thee the desires of thine heart.

⁵ Commit thy way unto the LORD; trust also in him; and he shall bring it to pass.

⁶ And he shall bring forth thy righteousness as the light, and thy judgment as the noonday.

⁷ Rest in the LORD, and wait patiently for him: fret not thyself because of him who prospereth in his way, because of the man who bringeth wicked devices to pass.

⁸ Cease from anger, and forsake wrath: fret not thyself in any wise to do evil.

⁹ For evildoers shall be cut off: but those that wait upon the LORD, they shall inherit the earth.

¹⁰ For yet a little while, and the wicked shall not be: yea, thou shalt diligently consider his place, and it shall not be.

¹¹ But the meek shall inherit the earth; and shall delight themselves in the abundance of peace.

¹² The wicked plotteth against the just, and gnasheth upon him with his teeth.

¹³ The LORD shall laugh at him: for he seeth that his day is coming.

¹⁴ The wicked have drawn out the sword, and have bent their bow, to cast down the poor and needy, and to slay such as be of upright conversation.

¹⁵ Their sword shall enter into their own heart, and their bows shall be broken.

¹⁶ A little that a righteous man hath is better than the riches of many wicked.

¹⁷ For the arms of the wicked shall be broken: but the LORD upholdeth the righteous.

¹⁸ The LORD knoweth the days of the upright: and their inheritance shall be for ever.

¹⁹ They shall not be ashamed in the evil time: and in the days of famine they shall be satisfied.

²⁰ But the wicked shall perish, and the enemies of the LORD shall be as the fat of lambs: they shall consume; into smoke shall they consume away.

²¹ The wicked borroweth, and payeth not again: but the righteous sheweth mercy, and giveth.

²² For such as be blessed of him shall inherit the earth; and they that be cursed of him shall be cut off.

²³ The steps of a good man are ordered by the LORD: and he delighteth in his way.

²⁴ Though he fall, he shall not be utterly cast down: for the LORD upholdeth him with his hand.

²⁵ I have been young, and now am old; yet have I not seen the righteous forsaken, nor his seed begging bread.

²⁶ He is ever merciful, and lendeth; and his seed is blessed.

²⁷ Depart from evil, and do good; and dwell for evermore.

²⁸ For the LORD loveth judgment, and forsaketh not his saints; they are preserved for ever: but the seed of the wicked shall be cut off.

²⁹ The righteous shall inherit the land, and dwell therein for ever.

³⁰ The mouth of the righteous speaketh wisdom, and his tongue talketh of judgment.

³¹ The law of his God is in his heart; none of his steps shall slide.

³² The wicked watcheth the righteous, and seeketh to slay him.

³³ The LORD will not leave him in his hand, nor condemn him when he is judged.

³⁴ Wait on the LORD, and keep his way, and he shall exalt thee to inherit the land: when the wicked are cut off, thou shalt see it.

³⁵ I have seen the wicked in great power, and spreading himself like a green bay tree.

³⁶ Yet he passed away, and, lo, he was not: yea, I sought him, but he could not be found.

³⁷ Mark the perfect man, and behold the upright: for the end of that man is peace.

³⁸ But the transgressors shall be destroyed together: the end of the wicked shall be cut off.

³⁹ But the salvation of the righteous is of the LORD: he is their strength in the time of trouble.

⁴⁰ And the LORD shall help them, and deliver them: he shall deliver them from the wicked, and save them, because they trust in him.

PURPOSE: A Guide to Righteous Living and How to Obtain God's Blessings

"Do not fret thyself (verses 1 and 8)..... but *depart from evil"* (verse 27).

This psalm is not a prayer but an instruction and teaching about godly wisdom.

Its theme concerns the believers' attitude towards the apparent success of the wicked and the hardship of the righteous (see *Psalms 49 and 73*).

Who are a righteous person and a wicked person?

The righteous person is the one who has turned away from evil and does good continually while the wicked on the other hand makes unjust gain, borrows with no plans to repay or return and plots evil against the righteous.

While the righteous will earn God's blessings, the wicked earns God's displeasure and wrath, hence they are cut off.

One major temptation which faces the Christians or believers today is being envious of the success, prosperity and fast progress of the worldly people. David being deeply concerned about the salvation of the believers who are the righteous, warned seriously in his teaching and instructions about godly living (*in this psalm 37*) that the worldly people who are the wicked should not be emulated. Why?

The wicked appear to be making great success, prospering and fast progressing in their plans and all their endeavors; all these success stories are always short lived as they (wicked) loose all they acquire on earth within a short time and they themselves come to a destructive end (*verse 10*).

The activities of the wicked are seen in verses 9, 12, 13, 14, 21 and 32. The wicked are always ready to kill, to steal and to destroy the soul which they cannot and do not create. They have no fear of God.

Result of wickedness

The reward for the wicked activities can be seen in verses 15, 17, 20 & 38.

In all the struggles of the wicked, their gain is destruction. The Psalmist made us to realize that in their folly, their fate is eternal condemnation. For instance, verse 15 says *"their sword shall enter into their own heart, their bows shall be broken"*. Verse

17also says, *"The arm of the wicked shall be broken"*. while verse 20 says, *"the wicked shall perish, into smoke shall they consume away"*.

We, as believers are therefore advised not to fret our selves (verse 1) because of evildoers and we should not be envious of them in any way for they (wicked) will only earn God's wrath.

Gods' Blessings

What then should a believer or Christian do to earn God's favor and blessings?

King David, the Psalmist counsels all believers and Christian to:

i. Delight themselves in the Lord (verse 4).
ii. Commit their ways into the hands of the Lord (verse 5).
iii. Rest in the Lord and wait patiently for him (verse 7).
iv. Cease from anger and forsake wrath (verse 8).
v. Depart from evil (verse 27)

This means that as believers, we should desire and enjoy the nearness of God's presence, the truth and the righteousness of His word (*Job 22:2b; 27:10; Isaiah 58:14*). We should also trust in the Lord and totally turn away from evil and do good always.

For the believers who delight and trust in God receive their reward from God; God grants the desires of their heart. This suffices to say that:

i. God will answer the cry of their hearts if their desires are in accordance with the will of God (*John 15:7*).

ii. When we delight ourselves in God and His will, He Himself places His desires within our hearts that He then sets out to fulfill them (*Philippians 2:13*).

Psalm 37:6 tells us that God shall bring forth righteousness as light. This means that the righteous man that is oppressed by the wicked will receive the following promises from God:

i. Answers to their prayers (*verses 4 to 5*).

ii. Vindication of their righteous standard (*verse 6*).

iii. A heavenly inheritance (*verses 9, 11, 34*).
iv. Receiving God's mercy and lending (*verse 2b*).
v. The Lord's sustaining help (*verses 17 to 19, 39*).
vi. Salvation (*verses 39, 40*).
vii. God's help, deliverance and safety (*verse. 40*).

However, in spite of God's promises above, this Psalm reveals how the righteous must react when the unrighteous prosper in spite of their evil and immoral ways.

We must steadfastly persevere in the faith while waiting for God to bring about justice and vindicate us (*Psalm 37:1; Psalm 73; Proverbs 3:31; 23:17; 24:1; Jeremiah 12*).

Patience while undergoing troubles or suffering is possible through the help of the Holy Spirit (*Galatians 5:2; Romans 8:3-4: Ephesians 4:1-2; Colossians 1:11; 3:12*) who assures us that God will reward the righteous and punish the wicked (*Romans 8:28; Hebrews 12:1-2, 5-13*).

Nevertheless, none is righteous except God, but when we come to the Lord Jesus Christ for the forgiveness of our sins, and we are cleansed in His blood, we become righteous in Him. Then we can claim the promise in verses 29 and 39 that the righteous shall inherit the land and dwell in there forever and that their salvation is from the Lord and He is their strength in times of trouble.

We must take cognizance of the fact that the salvation of our souls is the greatest thing that can happen to us. All the things we pursue on earth in the world such as material gains, position, power, recognition will one day perish. But those who trust in the Lord and delight in Him will live forever.

Will your pursuit on this earth stand the test of time?

Wait for the Lord and keep His ways (*verse 34*).

"Mark the perfect man, and behold the upright; for the end of that man is peace" (verse 37).

PRAYERS POINTS: Lord, help me never to envy the wicked.

Teach me God, to turn my eyes from the transient glory of the wicked in Jesus name.

Grant us, O Lord the steadfastness to hope in you till the end and to keep your ways and do your will in Jesus name.

CHAPTER THIRTY - EIGHT
THE PRAYER OF A SUFFERING PENITENT

BIBLE READING: PSALM 38 (King James Version)

O Lord, rebuke me not in thy wrath: neither chasten me in thy hot displeasure.

2 For thine arrows stick fast in me, and thy hand presseth me sore.

3 There is no soundness in my flesh because of thine anger; neither is there any rest in my bones because of my sin.

4 For mine iniquities are gone over mine head: as an heavy burden they are too heavy for me.

5 My wounds stink and are corrupt because of my foolishness.

6 I am troubled; I am bowed down greatly; I go mourning all the day long.

7 For my loins are filled with a loathsome disease: and there is no soundness in my flesh.

8 I am feeble and sore broken: I have roared by reason of the disquietness of my heart.

9 Lord, all my desire is before thee; and my groaning is not hid from thee.

10 My heart panteth, my strength faileth me: as for the light of mine eyes, it also is gone from me.

11 My lovers and my friends stand aloof from my sore; and my kinsmen stand afar off.

12 They also that seek after my life lay snares for me: and they that seek my hurt speak mischievous things, and imagine deceits all the day long.

13 But I, as a deaf man, heard not; and I was as a dumb man that openeth not his mouth.

14 Thus I was as a man that heareth not, and in whose mouth are no reproofs.

15 For in thee, O LORD, do I hope: thou wilt hear, O Lord my God.

16 For I said, Hear me, lest otherwise they should rejoice over me: when my foot slippeth, they magnify themselves against me.

17 For I am ready to halt, and my sorrow is continually before me.

18 For I will declare mine iniquity; I will be sorry for my sin.

19 But mine enemies are lively, and they are strong: and they that hate me wrongfully are multiplied.

20 They also that render evil for good are mine adversaries; because I follow the thing that good is.

21 Forsake me not, O LORD: O my God, be not far from me.

²² Make haste to help me, O Lord my salvation.

PURPOSE: - A Prayer for Help from God When Suffering or In Trouble

This Psalm is an anguished prayer for God to withdraw chastisement for sins committed. The greatest problem in the world is sin, sin when we go our own way as opposed to God's way.

Sin is a killer; for the bible in Romans 6:23a says, *"The wages of sin is death"*.

The Psalmist was burdened with his sin and greatly troubled in his spirit. He (David) is consumed with senses of God's displeasure (*verses 1-2*). He (David) was failing in strength and he knew that his suffering was as the result of his own foolish sins (*verses 3, 5*). He accepted his punishment, confessed his sins, and looked up to God for help and salvation (*verses 18, 21, 22*).

All who have sinned and who suffer from guilt, remorse and a sense of God's judgment will be able to identify with this prayer.

This Psalm can be divided into three parts each beginning with an address to God.

The burden of sin (Verses 1 to 8)

David expresses, without reservations, his inner feelings as he examines his life before God. There is an expression of guilt which suggests that his physical suffering was due to his sin (*verses 3, 5, 7 to 10*).

Loneliness resulting from sin (verses 11 to 14)

Sin often prevents free fellowship, especially where the sin affects personal relationship. Here David stated that in addition to the pains he was going through, his enemies were after him, even his loved ones and friends deserted him.

It is important, therefore, not only to confess our sins to God, but make restitution with those we have wronged.

In his desperation, David cried to God for he knew his deliverance could only come from God.

The confession of sin (*verse 15 to 22*)

David recognized that he could not deal personally with his sin. He therefore turned to the merciful God for salvation (Psalm 51). What great lesson for us all! This should be our attitude, not to focus on our sins but always to seek God's mercy.

When we are troubled by sin in our lives and other circumstances, we should run to the Lord in repentance and for his help. Man's help is unreliable and often disappointing. On the other hand God is able to deliver us from any situation that is beyond and against us. He is the answer to all problems and challenges. Trust and depend on him always, He does know and will never disappoint you.

Important facts to note by believers

There are two consequences of committing serious sin for a believer after knowing the Lord and having received His mercy.

i. Divine anger and judgment
ii. Body pains and mental anguish.

King David and Saul are examples of people who experienced the two consequences mentioned above.

The motion or belief that God always forgives and forgets sin without ever punishing the repentant or offender is not a biblical teaching and does not hold waters. A repentant sinner, after experiencing God's forgiveness will experience for some time there after the temporal consequence or punishment of their forgiven sins, sometimes after.

David a man after God's heart also was forgiven of his committed adultery with Uriah's wife and also the cold-blooded murder of Uriah. God showed His divine anger and judgment on David pronouncing *'the sword shall never depart from thine house'* (*II Samuel 12:10 - 19*).

The seed of David's union with Uriah's wife died and God in II Samuel 12:11 pronounced this punishment for David, saying *"I will raise up evil against thee out of thine own house, and I will take thy wives before thine eyes, and give them unto thy neighbour, and he shall lie with thy wives in the sight of this sun'*. In that story, we can see that God did not permit David to die but he allowed the child to die (II Samuel 12:14)..

Again, sin brings a heavy burden and suffering to the transgressors. God may allow as punishment severe sickness or even death as the result of our sin. See (*verses 3 to 10 of Psalm 38; I Corinthians 11:29-30*).

Deliberate or Willful Sins

Another fact to examine is the act of committing sin deliberately which is referred to as willful sin. That is, a sin one commits out of one owns free will. It is when you already know that what you are about to do is contrary to God's will or standard and you go ahead to do it. This also has its own consequences. The terrible consequence of deliberate or willful sin is the loss of God's fellowship and presence.

David felt the distance of God from him and needed God's fellowship. Hence, he pleaded with God not to be far away from him (*Psalm 38:21; 22:9; 35:22; and 71:12*).

It is a grievous and bitter experience to commit deliberate or willful sin after experiencing the mercy of God or being born-again and the indwelling of the Holy Spirit.

Beware of sin, it does not only kill and destroy but can separate you from the love of God.

Flee from all that is sinful be it willful or unwillful.

"Blessed is the man that walketh not in the counsel of the ungodly, nor standeth in the way of sinners nor sitteth in the seat of the scornful. But his delight is in the law of the Lord, and in his law doth he meditate day and might. And he shall be like a tree planted by the rivers of water, that bringeth forth his fruit in his season; and whatsoever he doeth shall prosper" (*Psalm 1: 1-3*)

PRAYER POINTS: Father, give me the grace and strengthen me mightily.

Let me be filled with the knowledge of your will in Jesus name.

LORD, inject in me the heavenly spiritual vitamins that will sustain me in evil days and do not be far from me in Jesus name.

CHAPTER THIRTY - NINE
THE BREVITY OF MAN'S LIFE SPAN

BIBLE READING: **PSALM 39 (King James Version)**

I said, I will take heed to my ways, that I sin not with my tongue: I will keep my mouth with a bridle, while the wicked is before me.

² I was dumb with silence, I held my peace, even from good; and my sorrow was stirred.

³ My heart was hot within me, while I was musing the fire burned: then spake I with my tongue,

⁴ LORD, make me to know mine end, and the measure of my days, what it is: that I may know how frail I am.

⁵ Behold, thou hast made my days as an handbreadth; and mine age is as nothing before thee: verily every man at his best state is altogether vanity. Selah.

⁶ Surely every man walketh in a vain shew: surely they are disquieted in vain: he heapeth up riches, and knoweth not who shall gather them.

⁷ And now, Lord, what wait I for? my hope is in thee.

⁸ Deliver me from all my transgressions: make me not the reproach of the foolish.

⁹ I was dumb, I opened not my mouth; because thou didst it.

¹⁰ Remove thy stroke away from me: I am consumed by the blow of thine hand.

¹¹ When thou with rebukes dost correct man for iniquity, thou makest his beauty to consume away like a moth: surely every man is vanity. Selah.

¹² Hear my prayer, O LORD, and give ear unto my cry; hold not thy peace at my tears: for I am a stranger with thee, and a sojourner, as all my fathers were.

¹³ O spare me, that I may recover strength, before I go hence, and be no more.

PURPOSE: - To serve as a checkers to how we conduct our earthly affairs

Psalm 39 is a continuation of the previous Psalm 38 which has its theme as "the prayer of a suffering penintent".

David, the Psalmist having been weighed down by the burden of his sin, felt he was still under the punishment of God. His realization that God is the one chastising him made him utter the words in verses 10, *"Remove thy stroke away from me; I am on some by the blow of thine hand"*.

This Psalm will be discussed under three sections, each holding a special interest for us.

Verses 1 to 3:

We live in a very wicked world and among people whose values are ungodly. They provoke us to discuss issues on various matters which include among others politics, religion, family and people in ways that are negative and unedifying. Hence the Psalmist, David, in his suffering makes a resolution to keep his mouth shut lest he speaks unadvisedly in the presence of the wrong company (*verse 1*). *"I will keep my mouth with a bridle, while the wicked is before me"*.

David was under heavy pressure with him.

Do you hold a bridle on your tongue?

Are you sufficiently careful about what you say, especially in the presence of unbelievers?

As God's children, we must be careful about what we say in the presence of people especially the wicked (James 1:26). We must let our speech be seasoned with salt (Colossians 4:6), we are to avoid careless talks for we shall one day give account of every word we utter.

Verses 4 to 11

The Psalmist here was conscious of the transient life (*verses 4 to 6*), so when he spoke, his focus was on the brevity of man's life and how that fact should affect the way we conduct our affairs. Any right thinking person, be it Christian or not cannot be blind to the fact that life on earth is very *brief* and that we are sojourners therein; heaven is our home for we shall die one day. That is why David prays that God will help him realize the brief span of his life on earth. (*verse 11; Psalm 62:9; 144:4; Job 7:7*). This should be the prayerful concern of every man especially the believer. God has given each one of us only a short time on earth as a period of testing to determine our faithfulness to God while living in the midst of a perverse generation opposed to God and His word.

It is therefore necessary for every one of us to search for the life that is eternal. That eternal life can only be received as a gift from God though faith in the Lord Jesus Christ.

"The free gift of God is eternal life in Christ Jesus our Lord" (*Romans 6:23b*)

Have you accepted this gift? If not, do so now. It is the best choice any man can make as it turns the brevity of life to ever-lasting life with God.

Verses 12 to 13

In these two verses, the Psalmist ends with a tearful plea to God to spare him from the judgment of His Holy eyes. He based his prayer on God's mercy (*Psalm 40:11*).

May all of us soberly learn to number our days so as to know the brevity of life (even at its longest) in relation to eternity and thereby to present to God a heart and life of wisdom.

Only what we do for God and others will endure forever (*Luke 12:20; James 4:14*).

"Lord, make me to know mine end, and the measure of my days, what it is; that I may know how frail I am" (*Psalm 39:4*)

PRAYER: Lord, help me to control my tongue and my utterance so that your name may be glorified in the name of Jesus.

Lord, teach me to number my days aright that I may gain a heart of wisdom in Jesus name.

Father, deliver me from all my transgressions and make me not the reproach of the foolish in Jesus name (verse 8).

CHAPTER FORTY
DELIGHT IN THE WILL OF THE LORD

BIBLE READING: **PSALM 40 (King James Version)**

I waited patiently for the LORD; and he inclined unto me, and heard my cry.

² He brought me up also out of an horrible pit, out of the miry clay, and set my feet upon a rock, and established my goings.

³ And he hath put a new song in my mouth, even praise unto our God: many shall see it, and fear, and shall trust in the LORD.

⁴ Blessed is that man that maketh the LORD his trust, and respecteth not the proud, nor such as turn aside to lies.

⁵ Many, O LORD my God, are thy wonderful works which thou hast done, and thy thoughts which are to us-ward: they cannot be reckoned up in order unto thee: if I would declare and speak of them, they are more than can be numbered.

⁶ Sacrifice and offering thou didst not desire; mine ears hast thou opened: burnt offering and sin offering hast thou not required.

⁷ Then said I, Lo, I come: in the volume of the book it is written of me,

⁸ *I delight to do thy will, O my God: yea, thy law is within my heart.*

⁹ *I have preached righteousness in the great congregation: lo, I have not refrained my lips, O LORD, thou knowest.*

¹⁰ *I have not hid thy righteousness within my heart; I have declared thy faithfulness and thy salvation: I have not concealed thy lovingkindness and thy truth from the great congregation.*

¹¹ *Withhold not thou thy tender mercies from me, O LORD: let thy lovingkindness and thy truth continually preserve me.*

¹² *For innumerable evils have compassed me about: mine iniquities have taken hold upon me, so that I am not able to look up; they are more than the hairs of mine head: therefore my heart faileth me.*

¹³ *Be pleased, O LORD, to deliver me: O LORD, make haste to help me.*

¹⁴ *Let them be ashamed and confounded together that seek after my soul to destroy it; let them be driven backward and put to shame that wish me evil.*

¹⁵ *Let them be desolate for a reward of their shame that say unto me, Aha, aha.*

¹⁶ *Let all those that seek thee rejoice and be glad in thee: let such as love thy salvation say continually, The LORD be magnified.*

¹⁷ But I am poor and needy; yet the Lord thinketh upon me: thou art my help and my deliverer; make no tarrying, O my God.

PURPOSE: - Praising and acknowledging God's goodness in sharing testimony to others.

This is a Psalm of dual themes. It is a good thing to gives thanks to the LORD Almighty (*Psalm 92:1-2*); and to also give testimony of the Lord's goodness to us.

David in Psalm 40 opens with a testimony of what the Lord has done for him (*verses 1 to 3*) and praised Him for His deliverance (*verse 5*).

David did not keep the goodness of God to himself, he shared what God had done for him willingly. He said *"And he hath put a new song in my mouth……."* (*verse 3*).

In verses 9 and 10, the Psalmist willingly described and shared what God had done for him telling the goodness of deliverance.

God is able to deliver His children who cry to Him when they are in distress. He rescues them and establishes their footsteps. God does that to enable us have a testimony and share with others His goodness. This will make those who do not know God to find Him.

Furthermore, what God has done for others gives us good encouragement **to** trust Him when our feet begin to slip as in verse 2.

It is important to let the world know the goodness of the Lord.

Do not be shy to give testimony of the Lord's goodness for it earns you more blessing and victory.

The True Worship: Delighting To Do Gods Will

Verse 8 Says *"I delight to do thy will"*

The Psalmist understood that the sacrifices and the symbolic rituals required by God in His law were inadequate by themselves and were no substitute for genuine commitment and obedience from the heart (*I Samuel 15:22; Isaiah 1:11-17; Jeremiah 7:22-23; Micah 6:6-8*).

Likewise, the believers of today may participate in baptism by immersion, Lord's Supper, various acts of worship, songs of praises, alms giving, evangelism, tithe payment and so on without a heart truly devoted to God and the commandment of His word. No religious ritual can compensate for the absence of the obedience that comes from faith (*Romans 1:5; Hebrews 10:1, 6*).

God's desire for each of us is to delight in doing His will and keeping His words within our hearts. That is why the Psalmist in verse 8 of this chapter declared that he delights to do God's will. Jesus Christ Himself declared His delight to do God's will and this is His motto (*Hebrews 10:7, 9 – 10*). Then said, "*Lo, I come to do thy will, O God*".

To do God's will is to have an 'open ear' (*verse 6*), meaning that we are to stand for willingness to learn and obey God's command and keep His words in our hearts. To achieve this, the need to read the Bible, meditate upon it and commune with God daily cannot be over emphasized. It is not possible to grow into a mature Christian or believer without a daily quiet time. We have to be aware of the fact that our walking with the Lord does not mean that our enemies will not attack us. When we experience such, we should cry to the Lord like David the Psalmist to make haste to help us. God will surely come to our rescue and frustrate the plans of our enemies against us as He did for David, Moses and others who delighted in His will.

Remember to delight and do His will for it is by Christ's obedience unto death that we are been sanctified (*Hebrews 10:10)* in order that the law of God may be put into our heart (*Hebrews 10:16*). Thus, every believer must also affirm these words of Christ in their lives. "*Lo, I come to do thy will O God*".

No religious ritual can compensate for the absence of the obedience that comes from faith (Romans1:5) which is absolute delight in His will.

"Sacrifice and offering thou didst not desire; mine ears hast thou opened: burnt offering and sin offering hast thou not required.

Then said I, "Lo, I come: in the volume of the book it is written of me,

"I delight to do thy will, O my God: yea, thy law is within my heart"(Psalm 40:6-8).

PRAYER: Lord, teach and help me to proclaim your faithfulness to all around me in Jesus' name. Amen

My father and my Lord, Teach me always to delight in your will.

Withhold not thou thy tender mercies from me, O Lord: Let thy loving kindness and thy truth continually preserve me (verse 11) in Jesus name. Amen.

CHAPTER FORTY - ONE
PROMISES TO THE AFFLICTED
(A Psalm of the Compassionate)

BIBLE READING: PSALM 41 (King James Version)

Blessed is he that considereth the poor: the LORD will deliver him in time of trouble.

² The LORD will preserve him, and keep him alive; and he shall be blessed upon the earth: and thou wilt not deliver him unto the will of his enemies.

³ The LORD will strengthen him upon the bed of languishing: thou wilt make all his bed in his sickness.

⁴ I said, LORD, be merciful unto me: heal my soul; for I have sinned against thee.

⁵ Mine enemies speak evil of me, When shall he die, and his name perish?

⁶ And if he come to see me, he speaketh vanity: his heart gathereth iniquity to itself; when he goeth abroad, he telleth it.

⁷ All that hate me whisper together against me: against me do they devise my hurt.

⁸ An evil disease, say they, cleaveth fast unto him: and now that he lieth he shall rise up no more.

⁹ Yea, mine own familiar friend, in whom I trusted, which did eat of my bread, hath lifted up his heel against me.

¹⁰ But thou, O LORD, be merciful unto me, and raise me up, that I may requite them.

¹¹ By this I know that thou favourest me, because mine enemy doth not triumph over me.

¹² And as for me, thou upholdest me in mine integrity, and settest me before thy face for ever.

¹³ Blessed be the LORD God of Israel from everlasting, and to everlasting. Amen, and Amen.

PURPOSE: -   A prayer for Healing

This Psalm is a prayer of a sick man who is the Psalmist on His sick bed surrounded by people who do not wish him well though pretend to be friendly.

The Psalmist who was severely ill was surrounded by what category of people? He was surrounded by enemies, rivals and even a close friend (verse 9) whispered that he was dying. This attitude shows a pretence and unfaithfulness from a close friend of whom he expects support, comfort, good news and binding-up of His (Psalmist) broken-heart as commanded by God in Isaiah 61:11.

This type of friend can be referred to as an "unfriendly friend".

May God, protect and deliver us from all known and unknown unfriendly friends in Jesus name. Amen.

In his devastated situation, the Psalmist called on God confidently for healing. What made him so confident that God would heal him?

The Bible has many things to say about God's concern for the poor. God has a special concern for the weak and helpless and He blesses those who show loving-kindness to the needy and poor. The Psalmist knew the above fact that God helps those who show "regard for the weak; because he had shown integrity in this. Thus, David, the Psalmist, confidently expected God to show mercy to him.

Jesus reflected this value when he said, *"Blessed are the merciful, for they will be shown mercy"* (*Matthew 5:7*).

Verses 1 to 3 of this Psalm 41 expatiate on this principle of blessedness.

Perhaps we have known the experience ourselves (*verse 9*) of betrayal by trusted friends, colleagues or even family members; remember that the Lord Jesus was not spared of this experience when Judas, one of His disciples betrayed Him. This known and described experience of our Lord Jesus Christ is an encouragement that He is with us at every level of our sufferings.

If we have shared God's pity for those in need, we can pray with confidence to God for deliverance when we are in trouble. God promises in this Psalm that: He will protect us from harm (verse 1); bless our lives, destroy the powers of Satan and our enemies and give us His presence and divine healing when we are sick (verse 2).

(For further study on this Psalm 40, you can read and delve into *Psalms 72:4 and 12; Deuteronomy 15:7-11; Proverbs 29:14; Isaiah 11:4; Jeremiah 22:16; Matthew 6:30*).

We enjoy claiming promises from the Bible but we should also endeavor to take care of the conditions attached to the promises we claim.

PRAYER POINTS: Father, strengthen and help me not to doubt you in times of trials and tribulation. Let me remain steadfast in the face of all odds, in Jesus' name. Amen.

Lord Jesus, fill me with the spirit of loyalty and integrity for your glory. Amen.

NOT A BENE: Pray always for the poor and helpless in your society, church and country and consider how you can help some of them.